TABLE OF CONTENTS

TITLE	STARRING	PAGE
Buck's Bad Dreams	Buck	1
Don't Fear the Doctor	Knute	33
Even Inks Need Friends	Inks	65
Just Flash	Flash	97
Keeping Your Cool	Broadway	129
Nothing but the Truth	Harvest	161
Super Dewey	Dewey	193
Sweet Tooth Bun	Bun	227
The First Step	Harmony	259
The Pirate Koostoe	Koostoe	291
Twin Trouble	Little Brushy and Little Fixit	323

Welcome to Midlandia!

Buck's Bad Dreams

A Tales of Midlandia Storybook

by Michael Scotto
illustrated by The Ink Circle

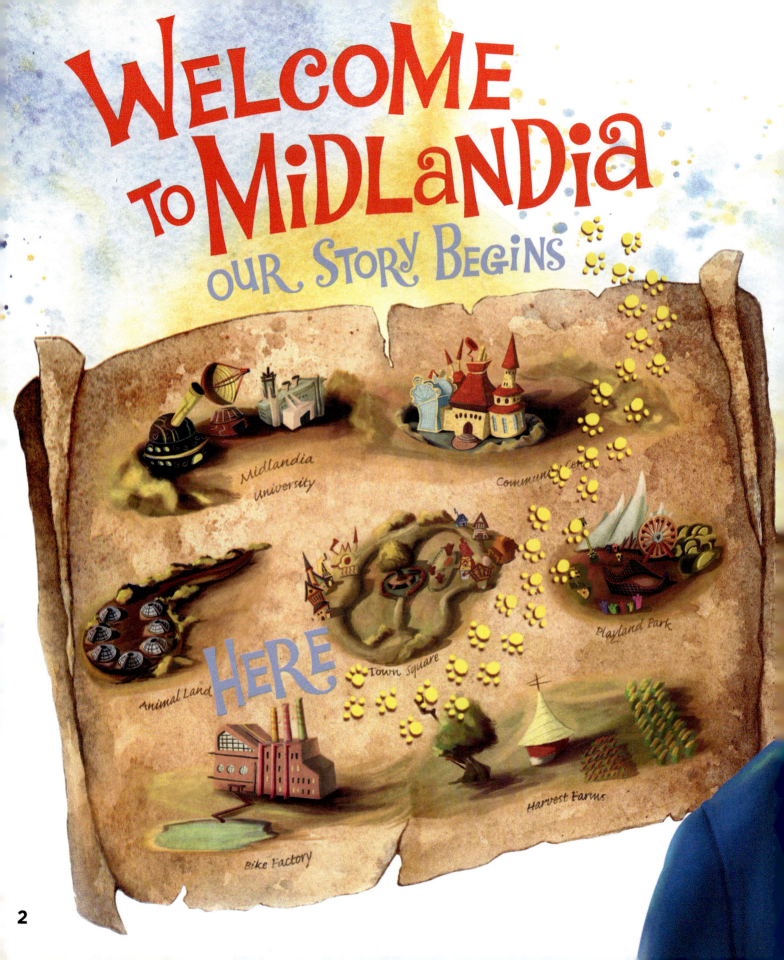

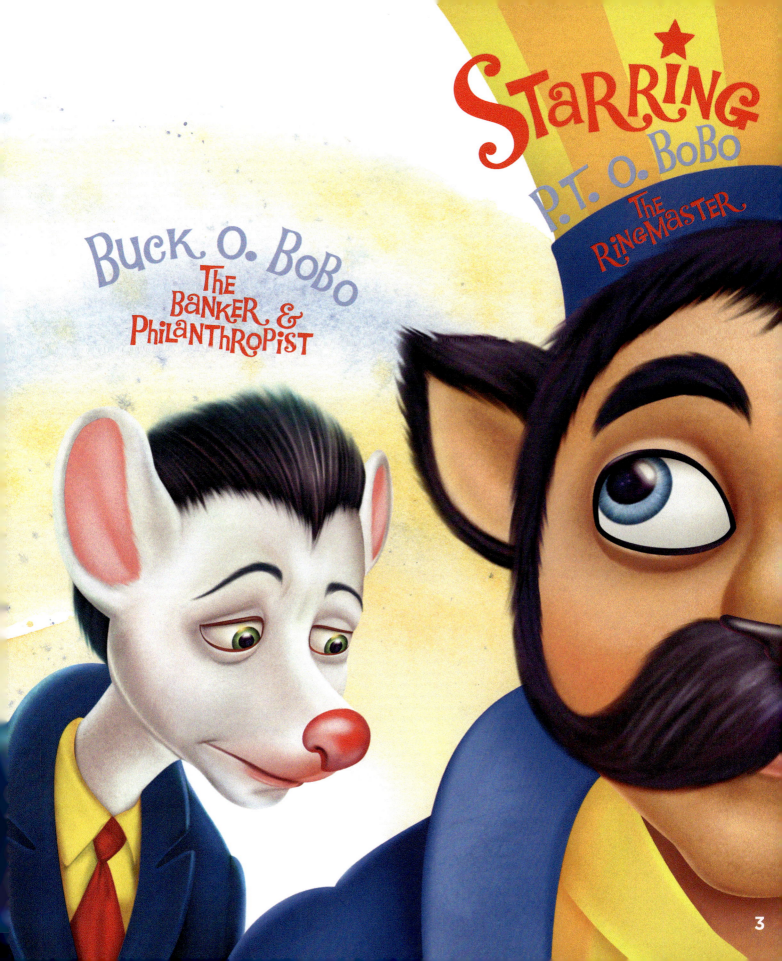

Buck's Bad Dreams

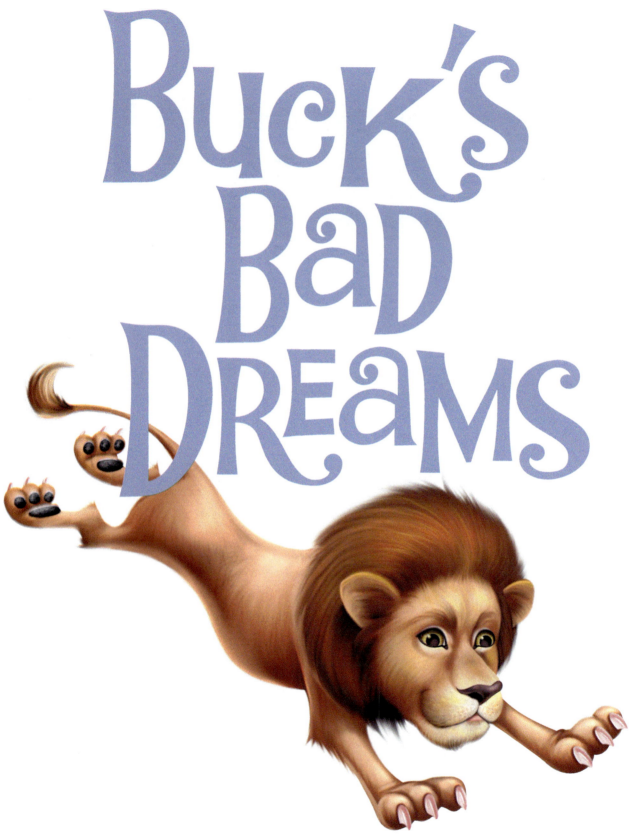

by Michael Scotto
illustrated by The Ink Circle

Buck the banker liked to give money back to his community, Midlandia. Those who care for and give back to their communities are called philanthropists.

Buck was proud to be a philanthropist. Partly, he liked having such a long and hard-to-spell title. He especially enjoyed signing letters. "Sincerely," he would write, "Buck O. Bobo, banker and **philanthropist**."

But even more, Buck enjoyed seeing Midlandians smile after he had helped them.

"**Thank you so much!**" said P.T., the circus owner. "With your donation, I can finally get that third ring for my next show!"

"I'll be in the front row on opening night," Buck promised.

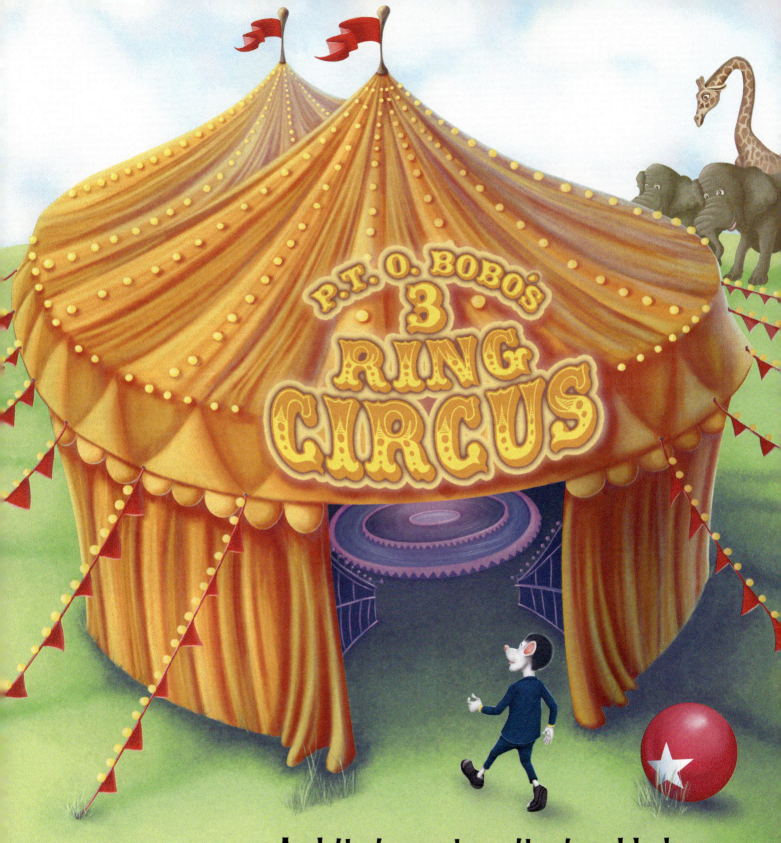

And that was how the trouble began.

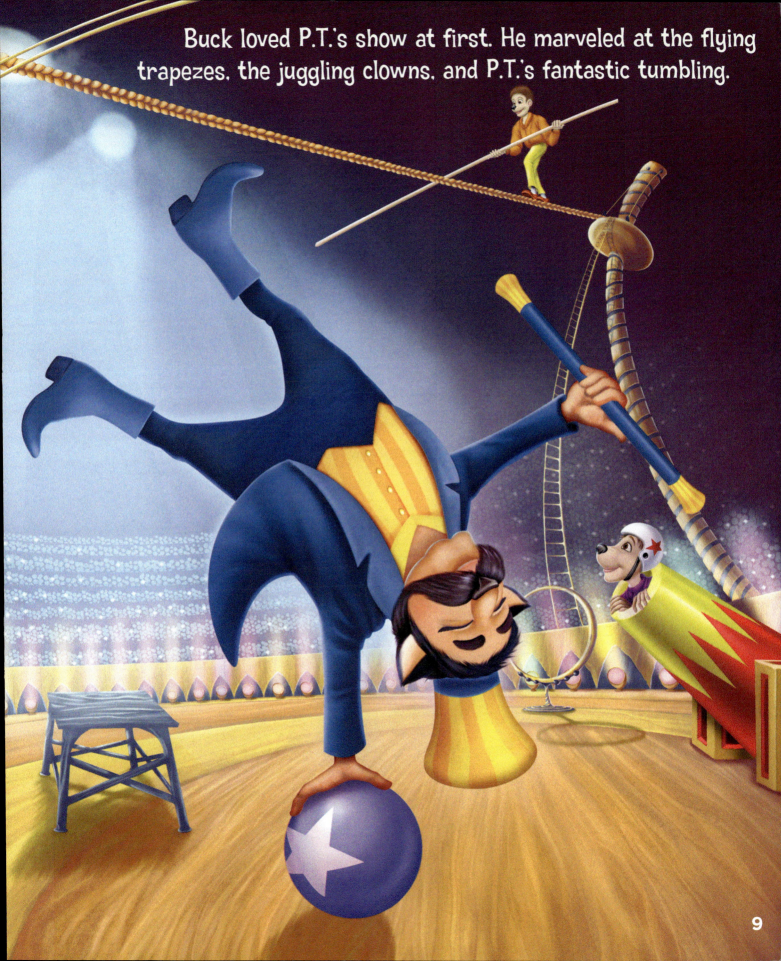
Buck loved P.T.'s show at first. He marveled at the flying trapezes, the juggling clowns, and P.T.'s fantastic tumbling.

But then....

"Ladies and gentle-Midlandians," P.T. announced, "I introduce our newest act, made possible by Mr. Buck O. Bobo! Please welcome to the center ring, **Larry the Leaping Lion!**"

The whole audience clapped wildly—everyone except for Buck. Buck was frozen with fear. *That lion is huge,* he thought. **He could swallow me whole!**

"Tonight," P.T. declared, "Larry will leap through the famed Hoop of Fire!"

The idea really scared Buck. He did not like fire one bit.

As the hoop burned, the lion jumped safely through. *He's coming right for me!* Buck thought. But the lion just trotted back to P.T. for a treat.

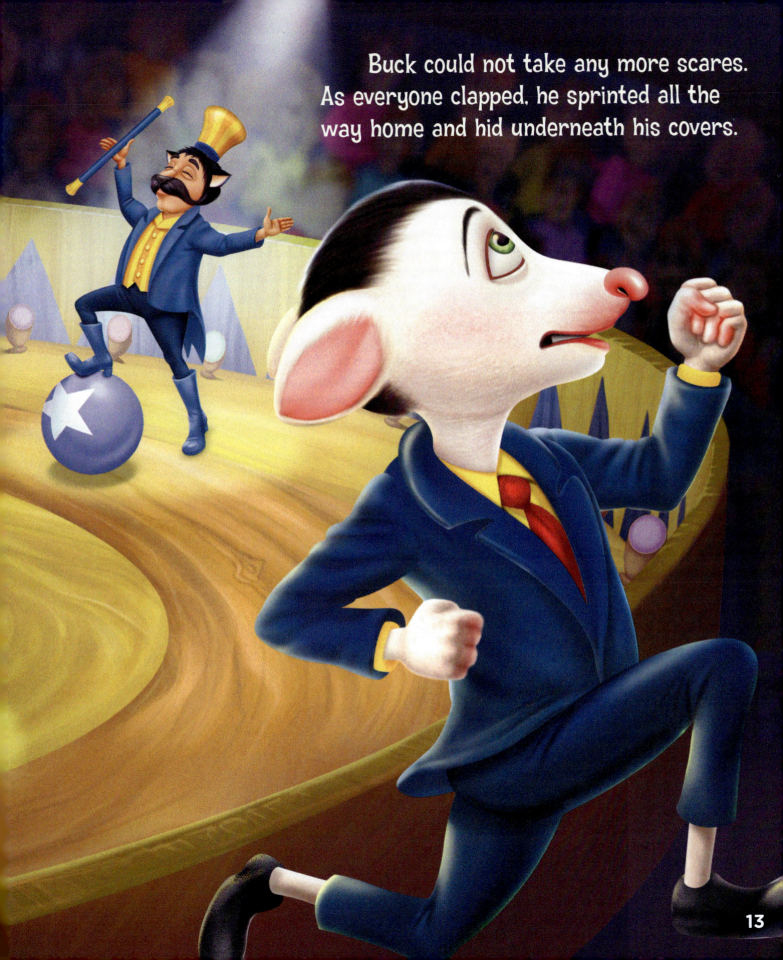

Buck could not take any more scares. As everyone clapped, he sprinted all the way home and hid underneath his covers.

That night, Buck heard a low growling sound. *How did I get here?* Buck thought, puzzled. *I went to sleep at home, but now I'm back at the circus!*

He heard the growling again.

It was P.T.'s lion! He was even bigger than before. Buck looked for somewhere to hide, and he saw something strange. *My bank vault!* he thought. *That looks safe.* He hurried for the vault, but out of nowhere, a ring of fire appeared in his way!

"I'm trapped," Buck whispered.

Just before the lion pounced...

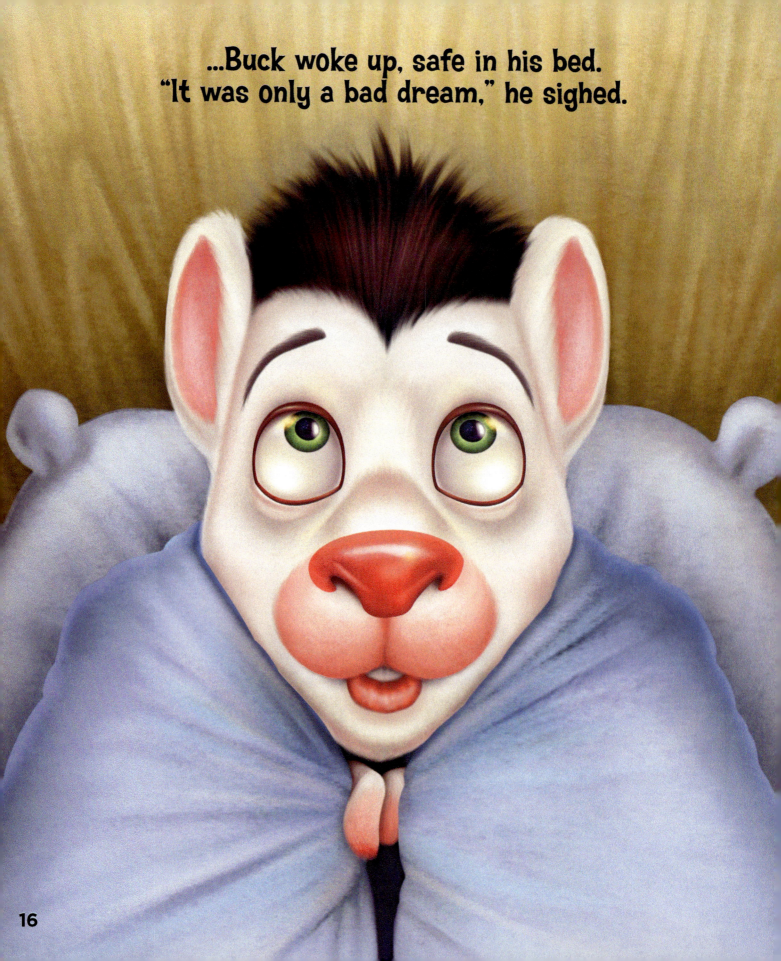

Buck was tired the next day—tired and grouchy. He had not slept a wink since his bad dream.

Soon, P.T. stopped by the bank to visit. "I missed you after the show," P.T. said. **"How did you like my new act?"**

Buck remembered his dream and suddenly grew very angry. "Your lion was lousy, and so was your show!" Buck yelled. **"In fact, I want my donation back."**

P.T. was shocked. "Without your help, I'll have to close the circus," he said.

"That's exactly the idea," Buck said.

After P.T. left, Buck felt guilty. He did not like hurting his friend. *If P.T.'s show is gone, though, maybe my bad dreams will go away, too,* he thought.

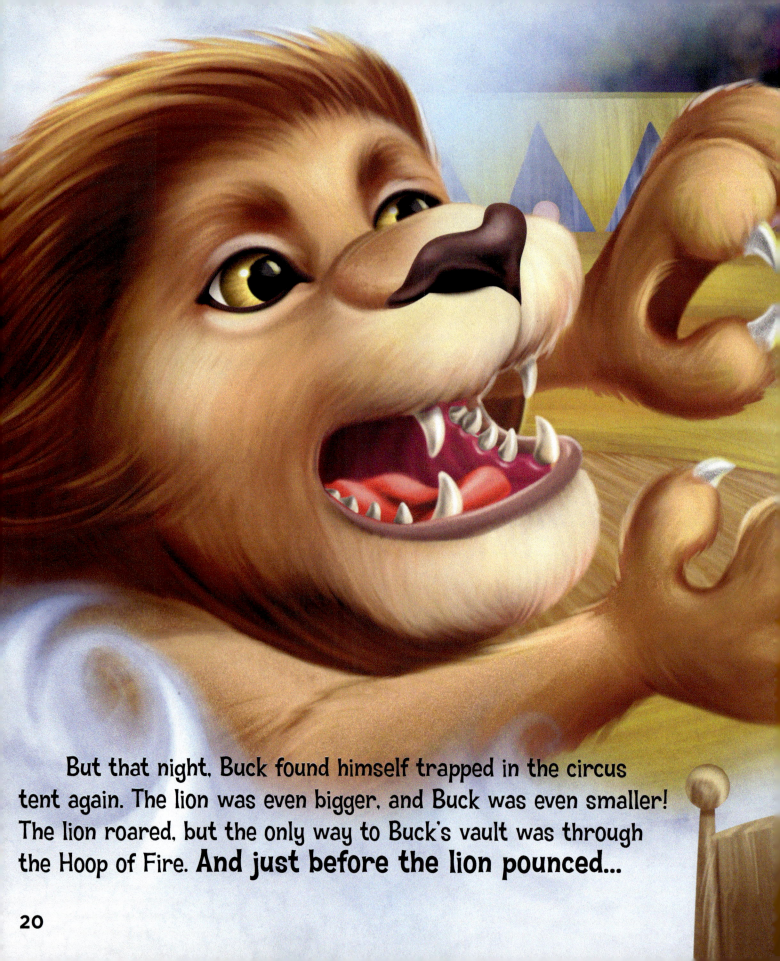

But that night, Buck found himself trapped in the circus tent again. The lion was even bigger, and Buck was even smaller! The lion roared, but the only way to Buck's vault was through the Hoop of Fire. **And just before the lion pounced...**

...Buck woke up shivering in his bed. "What is wrong with me?" he wondered.

In the morning, Buck went for a walk. "I don't get it," he said. "I made P.T. close his show, but I'm still having bad dreams." **Soon, he found himself at P.T.'s circus tent.**

Inside, Buck saw P.T. packing up.

"What are you doing here?" P.T. asked.

"I should not have made you close your show," Buck said. "I was not being a good philanthropist or a good friend. **I'm really sorry.**"

"Why did you get mad at me?" P.T. asked.

"Your circus lion really scared me," Buck admitted. "Then, I started having bad dreams about it, and I blamed you. I am so embarrassed."

"Bad dreams are nothing to be embarrassed about," P.T. said. "One time, I dreamt that I went out to perform wearing nothing but my underwear!"

"You have bad dreams?" Buck asked.

"Everyone has bad dreams sometimes," P.T. said. "Dreams come from things you see and things that you are thinking about. They are like stories that you make up without even knowing it. When you have a bad dream, you only need to change the story."

"How can I do that?" Buck asked.

"When you go to bed, think about fun things that you'd like to dream about—things that make you happy," P.T. suggested. "If you've had a bad dream, think about how you'd change it to make it a good dream. That usually helps me."

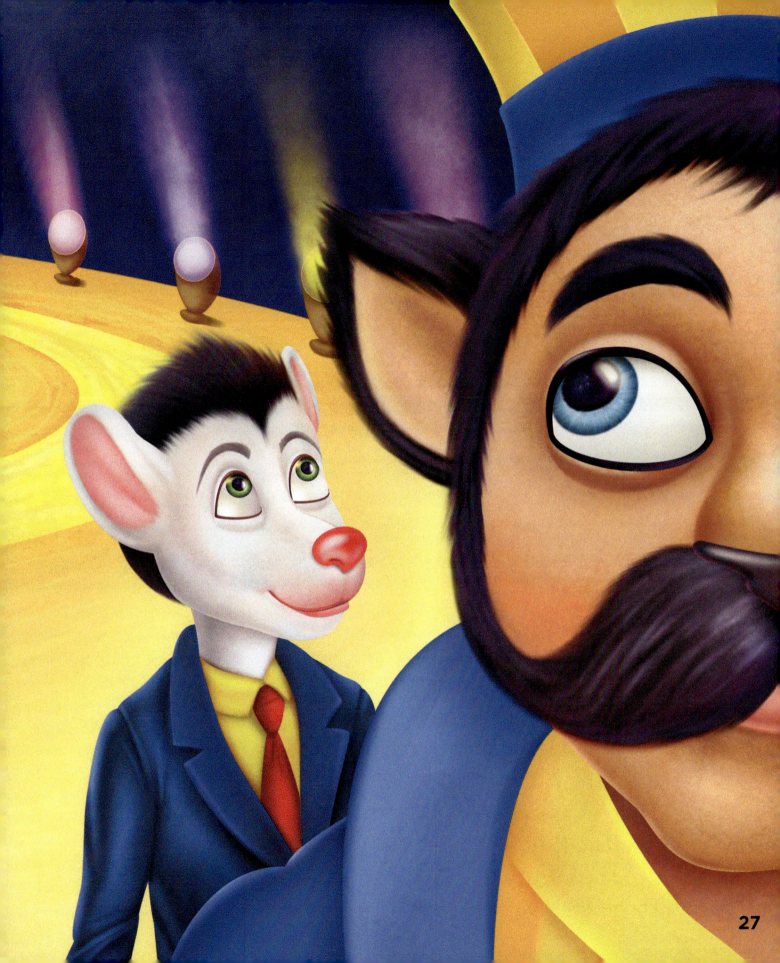

That night, Buck took P.T.'s advice. Soon, he found himself having another circus dream...but this time, it was a little different. Buck saw the Hoop of Fire, but he did not let it scare him. He just clapped his hands, and, in an instant, it turned into a ring of jewels and coins.

"**That's much better!**" Buck said as he jumped through the ring.

P.T.'s lion ran toward Buck. But as it got closer, Buck saw the lion shrink and turn into a lion cub before his eyes. The little cub jumped into Buck's arms. **"You aren't scary at all!"** Buck said as he petted the cub.

Buck could still hear the cub's purring when he woke. The moment he got to the bank, he sat down to write P.T. a thank-you note.

"Dear P.T.," Buck began. "**You were right.** I don't have to let bad dreams get me down. I'll come see your show again soon (but maybe not from the front row). Your friend, Buck O. Bobo." He smiled and then quickly added, "**banker and philanthropist.**"

Discussion Questions

Have you ever had a bad dream before?
What was your dream about?
Who helps you when you have bad dreams?

Philanthropists do not always give money to their communities. What are some other ways that you can contribute to the area where you live?

BUCK'S BAD DREAMS

Revised edition. First printing, January 2009.
Copyright 2020 © Lincoln Learning Solutions. All rights reserved.
294 Massachusetts Avenue
Rochester, PA 15074
Visit us on the web at http://www.lincolnlearningsolutions.org.
Midlandia® is a registered trademark of Lincoln Learning Solutions.

Edited by Ashley Mortimer
Character design by Evette Gabriel
Environmental design by Joshua Perry

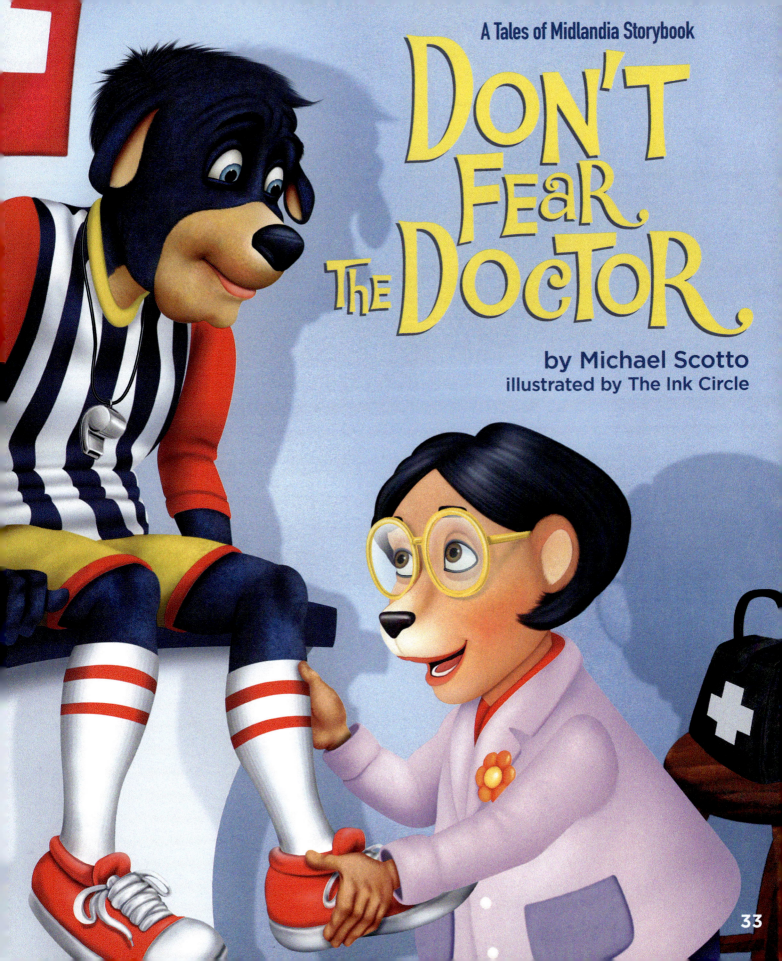

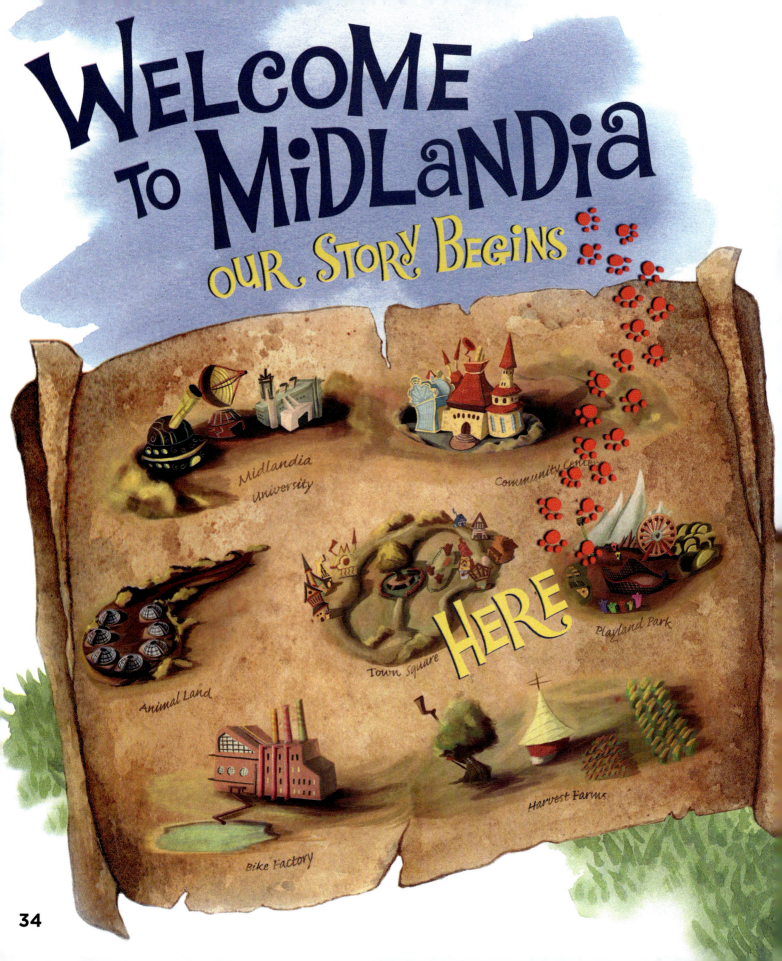

Starring

Knute O. Bobo
The Coach

Doc Fixit Wannadogood
The Doctor

Don't Fear the Doctor

by Michael Scotto
illustrated by The Ink Circle

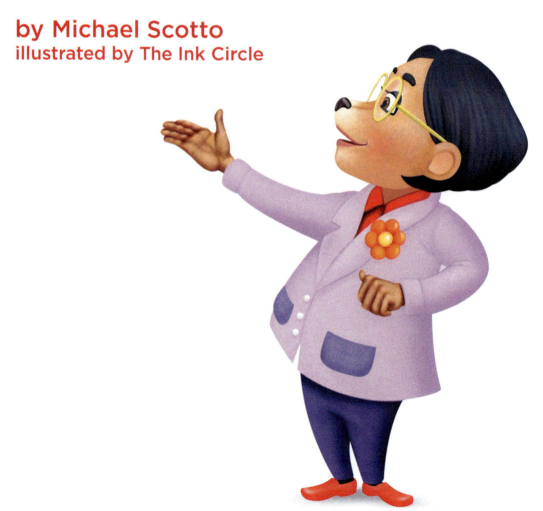

Coach was known as the toughest athlete in Midlandia. He watched over all of the games at Playland Park and made sure people played safely. **But sometimes, even coaches get hurt.**

Once, while refereeing a kickball game, Coach looked away just as Chief Tatupu launched the kickball with a mighty swing of his leg.
"**Look out, Coach!**" Chief shouted.
Coach turned back just in time to see the bright red kickball soaring right for his nose! He jumped out of the way at the last moment, landing with a crash.

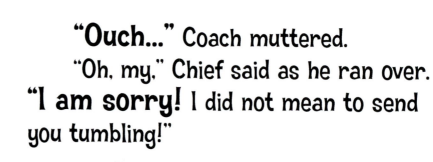

"Ouch..." Coach muttered.
"Oh, my," Chief said as he ran over.
"**I am sorry!** I did not mean to send you tumbling!"

"It's all right," Coach replied. "I live to tumble! I just bumped my ankle a little bit."

Chief helped Coach sit up. He then saw Coach's ankle. "You have bumped it more than a little bit." Chief said. "Your ankle is as red and puffy as the kickball! **You had better go see Doc Fixit."**

Coach did not respond.

"I know your ankle must hurt," Chief said. "If you go to Doc Fixit, she can give you medicine to help with the swelling, or maybe she can give you a shot."

"**A shot?**" Coach cried. He then grumbled so that no one would notice how worried he was.

"Go see the doctor, eh? I don't know about that. I think I'll just walk it off."

But when Coach tried to walk away, he just stumbled. "Owie!" he exclaimed.

"That is it," Chief said. "I am taking you to Doc Fixit, and there is nothing you can do about it."

Chief carried Coach on his back toward the Town Square. "You are not setting a very good example," Chief said. "You should not be so **stubborn**."

As the two neared the Town Square,
Coach made his move and jumped off Chief's back.
"I don't want to go to the doctor!" he declared.

"**Why are you scared?**" Chief asked. "You are the toughest athlete in Midlandia!"

"Even tough athletes can be scared," Coach said.

"I know," Chief said, "but there is no reason to be scared of the doctor."

"Do you know what it's like at the doctor's office?" Coach hissed.

"They have this big flashlight they point right at your eyes...

...and they hit you in the knees with a

GIANT hammer...

...and they poke at you...and those needles they have..." Coach shuddered. **"I don't like needles."**

"Have you ever been to the doctor?" Chief asked. "I have a check-up twice every year. Doc Fixit is a **nice** woman and a **good** doctor."

"Yeah, sure," Coach said. "That's what everybody says."

When Coach and Chief stepped into the office, they were greeted by a smiling, cheerful Doc Fixit.

"What seems to be the trouble today?" Doc asked.

"I'm fine," Coach said.

"He means," Chief said, "that he fell and hurt his ankle. Can you take a look?"

"First," Doc said, "let's make sure you didn't hurt your head when you fell. I'm going to use this **little** light to check your eyes, okay?"

"That little thing?" Coach asked. "**Sure. That doesn't seem so bad.**"

Doc shined the little light near Coach's eyes. "**Your eyes are fine,**" she said, "but your ears! My goodness, you need to clean them out, Coach!"

"Now let's test your reflexes to make sure you didn't hurt any other part of your leg." Doc took out a small rubber mallet. "I'm going to tap your knee with this."

The first part didn't hurt at all, so Coach said, "Okay...just not too hard."

Doc tapped Coach's knee, and his leg bounced up. "Wow!" Coach said. "Do that again!"

"Now, Coach," Doc said with a smile, "I'm going to touch your ankle very lightly, and you tell me where it hurts. **Is that okay?**"

"Yeah, I guess," Coach told her.

"Ooh!" Coach said. That part did hurt a little bit, but it still wasn't nearly as bad as he'd thought it would be.

"Just as I suspected," Doc said. "It's not broken; it's just twisted. You are going to need a shot to take down the swelling, though."

"**A shot!**" Coach shrieked. "Oh, no! I'm done for."

"It's really not so bad," Doc said. "It's just a little...what's that over there?" Doc pointed to the other side of the room.

While Coach looked away, she quickly gave him his shot.

Coach felt a little poke, and he looked back to Doc. "What was that little poke?" he asked.

Doc held up her needle. "**Congratulations, Coach,**" she said, "you've just had your first shot."

"You mean you did it already?" Coach cried.

The swelling started to go down right away.
Coach looked at Chief. "I can't believe it!" Coach said. "I barely felt it."
"Keep off that ankle for a couple of days," Doc said, "and you'll be better in no time."

Chief helped Coach down the road toward his house.

"All this time, I've been scared of the doctor, and there was no reason at all!" Coach said.

"I am glad you can see that doctors are here **to help you, not scare you,**" Chief said.

A few days later, Coach was back in action on the field. From then on, he always made sure that if someone got hurt at Playland Park, they went to the right place: **straight to the doctor.**

Discussion Questions

Can you think of a time when you were afraid of something, but you overcame your fears? What did you learn?

Have you ever been hurt or sick? How did a doctor help?

DON'T FEAR THE DOCTOR

Revised edition. First printing, January 2008.
Copyright 2020 © Lincoln Learning Solutions. All rights reserved.
294 Massachusetts Avenue
Rochester, PA 15074
Visit us on the web at http://www.lincolnlearningsolutions.org.
Midlandia® is a registered trademark of Lincoln Learning Solutions.

Edited by Ashley Mortimer
Character design by Evette Gabriel
Environmental design by Joshua Perry

A Tales of Midlandia Storybook

Even Inks Need Friends

by Michael Scotto
illustrated by The Ink Circle

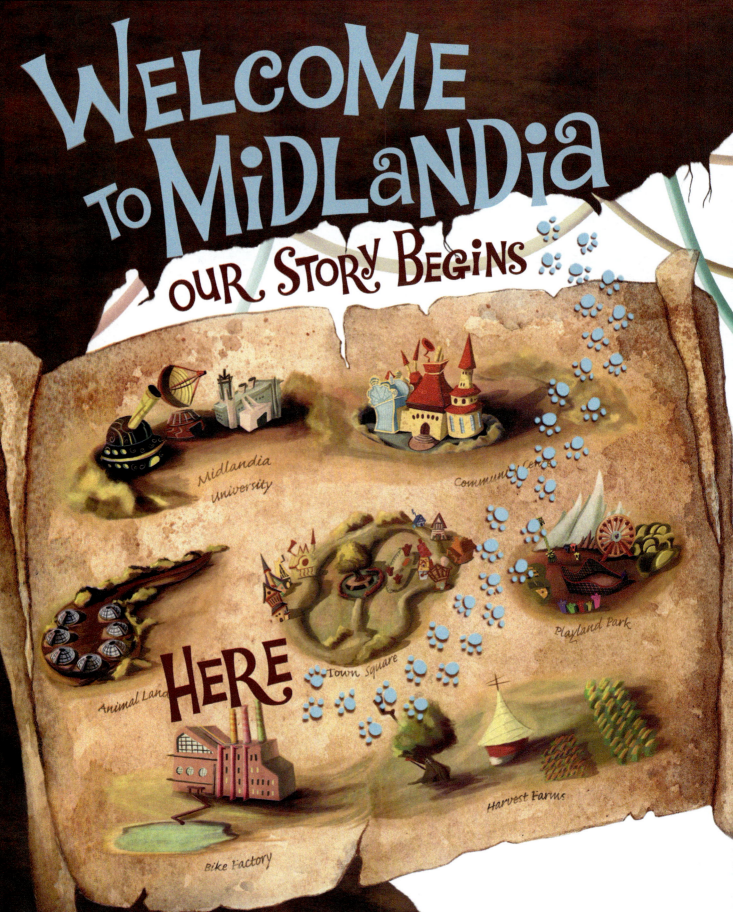

Even Inks Need Friends

by Michael Scotto
illustrated by The Ink Circle

Midlandia looked like the perfect town,

and in many ways, it was. Its hills were beautiful. Its citizens, the Midlandians, were hard-working and happy. But Midlandia did have a problem. Deep underground, beneath the surface...

...lived the Inks! The Inks were not hard-working. They spent all of their time playing.

But for the Inks, "playing" meant playing tricks on the Midlandians.

"**Help!**" cried Buck the banker. "Those Inks have caught my foot in a rope!"

"Oh, yuck!" cried Brick the builder. "Those Inks have filled my hard hat with mud."

Every week, the Inks would gather and plan new pranks to play.

"Let's go to the art gallery," said one, "and make Ink prints on the paintings."

"Let's sneak into the library," said another, "and turn the books all topsy-turvy!"

But the eldest Ink was not impressed. "These are tricks we've played before," he answered with a snort.

Then, something odd happened. An Ink who had never spoken before—a quiet, shy little Ink—decided to pipe up. "I have an idea," he said, "one that would shock the socks off those Midlandians!"

The others' ears perked up on end. They all leaned in to listen. "What if..." began the shy Ink. "What if we creep into town in the darkest of night and do something...nice?"

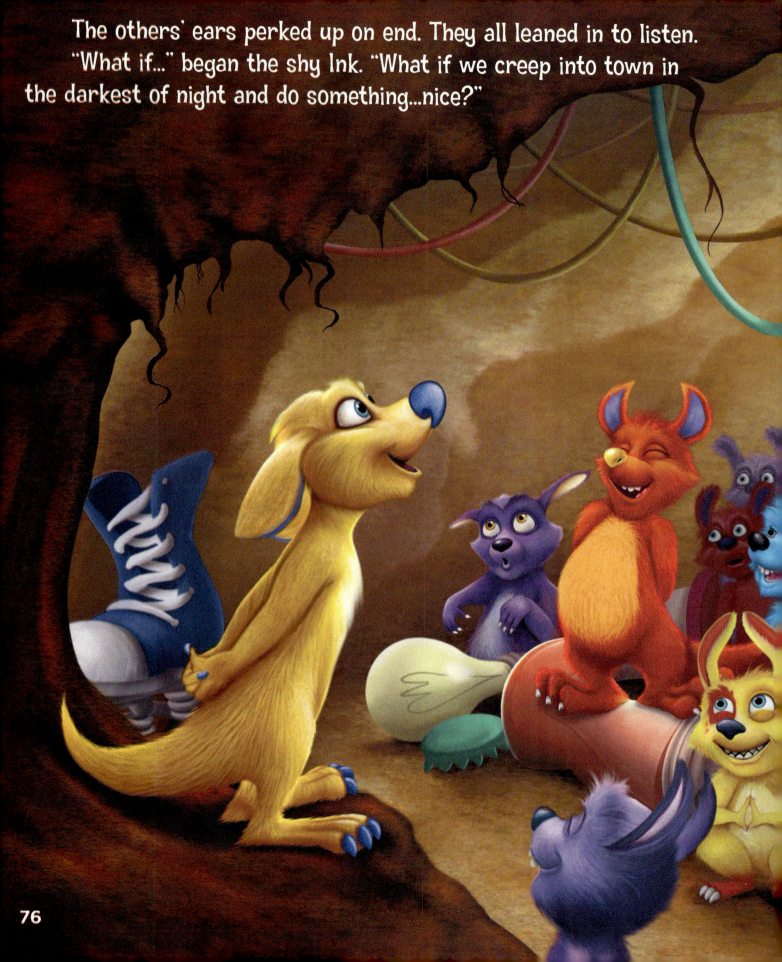

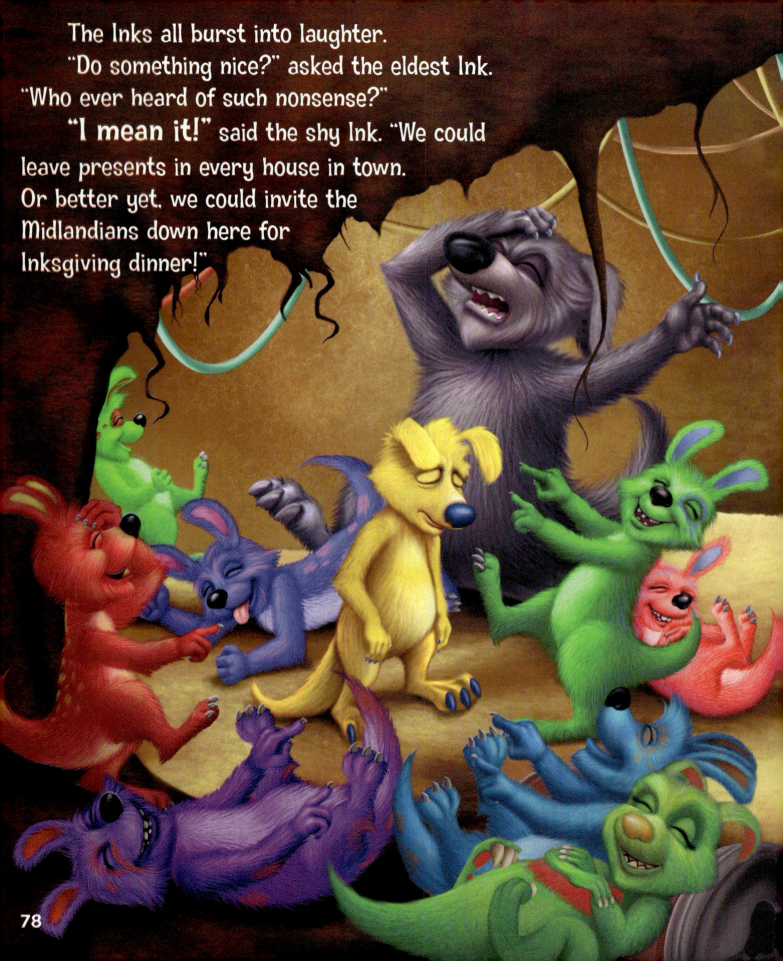

The Inks all burst into laughter. "Do something nice?" asked the eldest Ink. "Who ever heard of such nonsense?"

"I mean it!" said the shy Ink. "We could leave presents in every house in town. Or better yet, we could invite the Midlandians down here for Inksgiving dinner!"

The eldest Ink became very upset. "**Stop that, you!**" he shouted. "I will not have such talk in my cave. We are Inks, and Inks are not nice! If you can't say something mean, then don't say anything at all."

"Who says we always have to be mean?" asked the shy Ink.

The eldest Ink did not have a good answer, so he grew steaming mad. "**Out!**" he roared. "Get out! You are banished from this place."

"Banished?" asked the shy Ink.
"Banished!" the eldest Ink repeated. "That means you are no longer welcome here. Get your things and go now."

The shy Ink wandered sadly through the cold, rainy Town Square. He already missed his Ink friends, and he had nowhere to stay.

Soon, the Ink saw a sign he could read. "Animal Land," he read with a shiver. "I am like an animal... maybe I can stay here." And into Animal Land he crept.

Early the next morning, Wilda the zookeeper came to work. *There is so much to do!* she thought. *There are animals to feed, plants to care for, tours to give.... I'll start by feeding the lizards.*
Wilda opened the pantry door and saw every animal's food right where it belonged. But she also saw something that didn't belong.

"An Ink!" Wilda screamed. The Ink arched his back, as if ready to attack.

To Wilda's surprise, the Ink just let out a sneeze. "Excuse me!" he said. "I'm sorry to intrude like this, but...achoo!" The Ink sniffled. "May I please explain?"

Wilda gave the Ink some hot soup and a tissue for his stuffy nose. *This is an Ink of a different color,* she thought as he finished telling his story.

"I miss my friends, but I can't go home," said the Ink. **"Will you be my friend?"**

Wilda felt sorry for the poor little fellow, but she was still not sure if she could trust him. He was, after all, an Ink. "I don't know if Midlandians and Inks can be friends," she said.

"Well, then," said the Ink, **"do you need a helper?"**

Wilda decided to give the Ink a chance. "You can be my assistant for the day," she said. "Let's begin by feeding these iguanas."

"I'm not going near those things!" shrieked the Ink. "They'll swallow me whole!"

"Don't worry, little Ink," Wilda explained. "Iguanas might look scary, but they only like vegetables."

The Ink helped Wilda feed every lizard, bird, and fish in record time.

What a wonderful helper! Wilda thought. *But where has he gone now?*

The Ink reappeared holding a beautiful bunch of flowers. "I picked you the prettiest ones I could find!" he said.

But Wilda pinched her nose. "They're quite lovely," she said, "but boy, are they stinky!"

"I can't smell a thing," replied the Ink.

"That's because you have a cold, silly!" said Wilda. "It was a nice thought...but pee-eww!"

Soon, the zoo was ready to open for visitors.

"Thanks for your help," said Wilda.

"I'd be happy to stay as your assistant," offered the Ink.

"I have a better idea," Wilda replied. "Why don't you stay as my friend?"

"Really?" asked the Ink with a smile.

"My only problem now is...how will I explain this to everyone else?" wondered Wilda.

"That could be hard," agreed the Ink. "But you could try telling them this."

"Not everything can be known at first look.
You can't read one page and know the whole book.
Cute things can be mean and scary things nice.
That's why it's good to always look twice.
What I knew at the start has changed by the end,
And that's why this Ink is now my new friend."

Discussion Questions

Have you made any new friends this year? How did you meet?

What was the last thing that made you feel surprised? Why did it surprise you?

EVEN INKS NEED FRIENDS

Revised edition. First printing, January 2010.
Copyright 2020 © Lincoln Learning Solutions. All rights reserved.
294 Massachusetts Avenue
Rochester, PA 15074
Visit us on the web at http://www.lincolnlearningsolutions.org.
Midlandia® is a registered trademark of Lincoln Learning Solutions.

Edited by Ashley Mortimer
Character design by Evette Gabriel
Environmental design by Joshua Perry

Just Flash

by Michael Scotto
illustrated by The Ink Circle

A Tales of Midlandia Storybook

Starring

Flash
A Most Unusual Animal

Just Flash

by Michael Scotto
illustrated by The Ink Circle

No one in Midlandia really knew about Flash, not for sure. Nobody could figure out exactly what kind of animal he was. Not even Wilda, the zookeeper at Animal Land, was certain. Visitors would always ask her, "What do you call that big blue whatsit?" And Wilda could never answer.

"Well..." she would begin, "he's just Flash. No more, no less."

"He's strange!" the visitors always said.

Strange, weird, different: Flash heard all the ways Midlandians described him. He could not speak, but he could think and feel...and the Midlandians' words made him feel quite crummy.

Flash did not want to be strange, weird, or even different. *I only want to fit in*, he thought. But there was a problem: There were no other animals like Flash!

One day, Flash got an idea: He would simply become a different animal. *But which animal am I to be?* he wondered. That was the question.

Flash watched a herd of gazelles at play. *They are having so much fun!* he thought. **Maybe I can be a gazelle.**

But life with the gazelles did not really fit Flash. They were just too fast. They ran and hopped in circles and played ring-around-the-Flash.

After Flash left the gazelles, he saw a group of giraffes. *They seem so relaxed,* Flash thought. **Maybe I can be a giraffe.**

But he soon realized that he had picked the wrong spot. **They were just too mean.** They teased Flash about his short neck. To make matters worse, they flicked him on the nose with their tails and made Flash sneeze!

Flash felt ready to give up. But then, he discovered a family of zebras. They were sipping from a brook near the tall grass. **Check out those cool haircuts!** Flash thought. *I'll be a zebra...that's the life for me.*

The zebras did not run in circles around Flash. The zebras did not tease him either. They just ignored him altogether. Somehow, that made Flash feel even crummier than before.

I must have the wrong stripes, Flash finally decided. *That should be easy to fix.* Little did Flash know that changing one's stripes is always harder than expected.

First, Flash sneaked to the aquarium to have the squids squirt him with ink. But he and the squids could not see eye to eye.

Then, he tried to get some of the snakes to help...
until he remembered that he was **scared of snakes.**

The other animals were no help, so Flash finally decided to roll in the mud. Then, he crushed up some white daisies and rolled in those, too.

True, he smelled a little funny, but he had changed his stripes! *I look zebra-tastic!* he thought.

When Flash came around again, though, the zebras scooted even farther away than before. *They must not like my haircut,* he thought.

Flash tried to style his hair with a honeycomb...but the bees told him to **buzz off.**

Flash dived into the zebras' brook to hide. *The coast is clear,* he thought. **But when he crawled out of the water...**

...all of his hard work had washed away.
He was back to being weird, strange, different old Flash.

Then, Flash heard a visitor talking to Wilda. It was Badge, the sheriff of Midlandia. She loved to spend what little free time she had at Animal Land.

"What do you call that big blue whatsit?" Badge asked.

"Well..." Wilda began, "he's just Flash. No more, no less."

And no friends, Flash thought sadly. He wished he could turn invisible.

Badge did not mean someone else. Soon, she was helping Wilda feed Flash his favorite meal of oats. "You are different from any animal I have ever seen," Badge told Flash. Flash bowed his head, and Badge could tell he was embarrassed.

"**No, no...don't be ashamed!**" Badge said. "***Different*** isn't a dirty word, you know. Everyone is a little bit different, whether you're a fish, a Flash, or even a Midlandian. No matter what anyone else says, the things that make you different are the things that make you special."

For the first time, Flash really did feel special.

That night, as Badge headed for the exit, Flash tried to sneak out behind her.

"Oh, no, Flash," Wilda said. "Badge is a very busy Midlandian! She wouldn't have time to take care of you."

Please, Badge, please take me with you! Flash thought.
"If Flash really wants to stay with me." Badge said. "I'd be happy to care for him."
Flash lifted his head high and smiled.

Flash went to live with Badge. He helped her keep Midlandia safe, and she fed him oats, petted his nose, and brushed his coat.

Flash never did learn what kind of animal he was, not for sure. Instead, he learned something much more important—it simply did not matter. *I'm just Flash,* he thought.

No more, no less.

Discussion Questions

Have you ever had a hard time fitting in with a group? How did you handle it?

Name one thing about you that makes you unique or special.

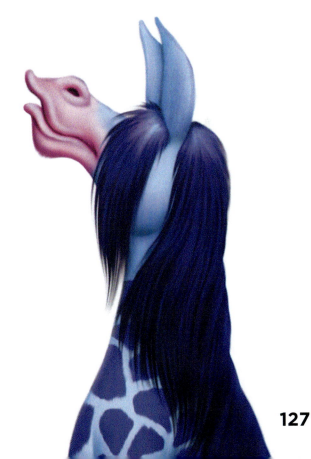

JUST FLASH

Revised edition. First printing, January 2012.
Copyright 2020 © Lincoln Learning Solutions. All rights reserved.
294 Massachusetts Avenue
Rochester, PA 15074
Visit us on the web at http://www.lincolnlearningsolutions.org.
Midlandia® is a registered trademark of Lincoln Learning Solutions.

Edited by Ashley Mortimer
Midlandian Map by Danielle Caruso

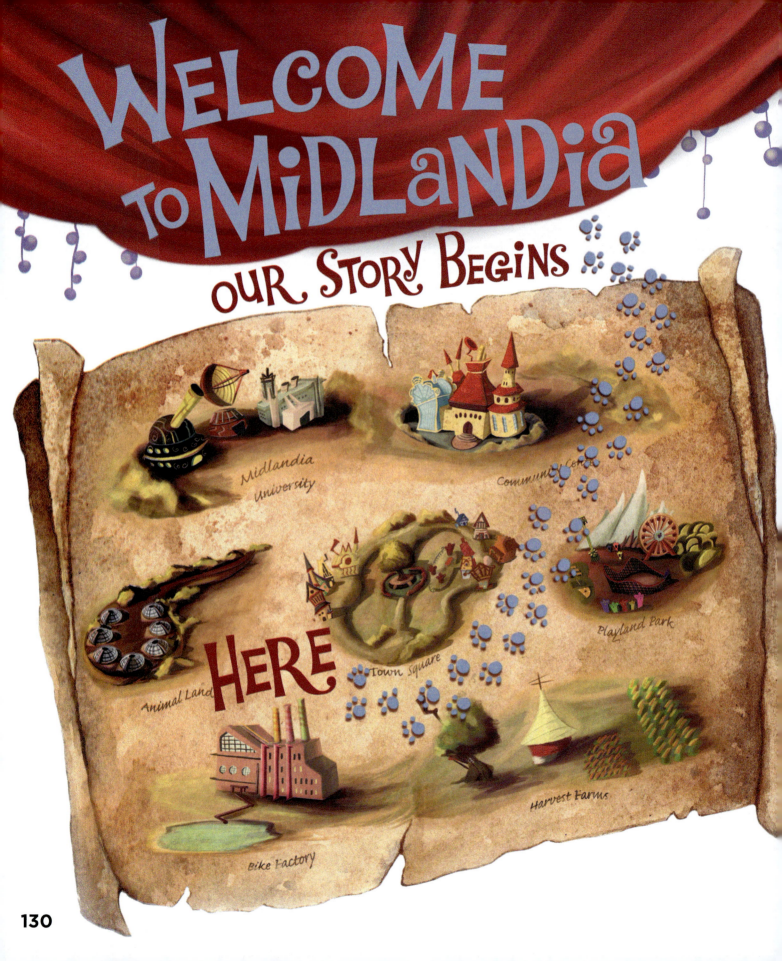

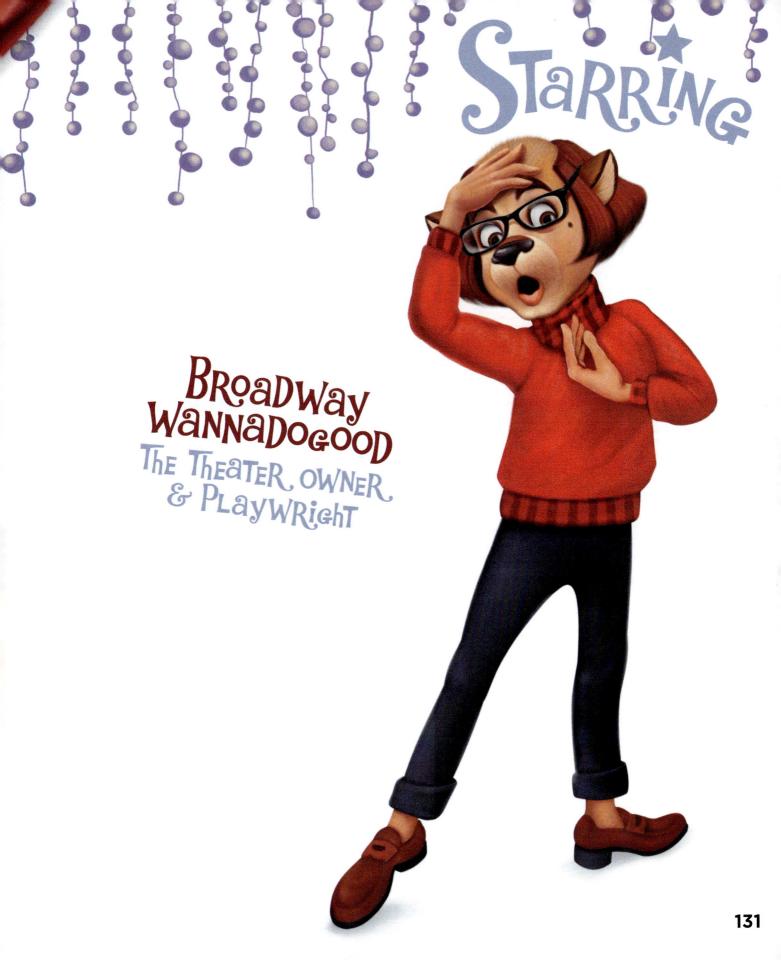

Keeping Your Cool

by Michael Scotto
illustrated by The Ink Circle

Broadway owned the Portal Theater in Midlandia. At his theater, Broadway wrote and directed plays for everyone to enjoy.

Broadway kept a close eye on every detail of his plays. He had to be sure that everything turned out just how he wanted. "I loved the way you said that line, Beaker," he said. "However, try it again, just a touch quieter. That will be much more dramatic."

Everyone tried to do exactly as Broadway said, because if they did not....

"No, no, no!" Broadway hollered. "That was too slow! I said a little slower, not slow like a turtle! I can't believe this!"

Broadway had an awful temper. "Nobody ever listens!" he cried, stomping his feet. **"It's a tragedy!** It could make a Midlandian weep. In fact, that's just what I'll do!"

After Broadway had calmed down, he noticed that his tummy was grumbling. *Boy, all that jumping around made me hungry!* he thought.

Broadway decided to stop for his favorite snack: a blueberry muffin at his friend Bun's bakery.

Broadway reached the counter. "One blueberry muffin, please!" he said.
Bun gulped nervously. "I'm sorry, Broadway," he stammered. "I just sold my last one."

Broadway could not believe his ears! "You're out of blueberry muffins?" he asked.

Bun nodded nervously. He knew that when Broadway lost his temper, he could be very tough to handle. "If you like...I do have some banana muffins," Bun suggested. "Perhaps you might enjoy something new."

That really got Broadway steamed. He felt his face getting hot. **"But I didn't come for something new!"** he yelled.

Meanwhile, Harmony watched from her table. She was a musician, and Broadway let her play shows at his theater.

"Uh-oh..." Harmony whispered. She knew what was coming next.

In the blink of an eye, Broadway jumped onto the counter and started toppling things over like an angry whirlwind. "I just want my blueberry muffin!" he howled. **"This is a tragedy!"**

As Broadway stamped his feet, he felt a hand touch his ankle. It was Harmony! "Can we go somewhere and talk?" she asked.

Harmony and Broadway sat together in the park. Broadway was no longer mad—he was worried.

"**Oh, gracious,** I was really rude to Bun," he said. "I am so embarrassed."

"Why do you think you got so upset?" asked Harmony.

"I just get so frustrated when things don't go my way," Broadway replied. "I try not to get upset, but I feel like I can never hold my temper in!"

"Everybody feels upset, disappointed, or even angry sometimes," Harmony said. "But losing your temper is never a good idea. It can be scary, and it is hurtful to others. Would you like to know how I keep my cool?"

"I would love to know," Broadway replied.

"When I think I might lose my temper," Harmony said, "I like to count to ten. It gives me time to calm down."

"I don't know, Harmony," Broadway said. "With my temper, I might need to count to a million. Do you have any other ideas?"

"How about this?" Harmony said. "Sometimes, when I'm upset, it helps me to think of things that make me laugh or smile. What makes you smile?"

"I always smile when I think about my theater," Broadway said. "After each show, I get to come out and take a bow. Everybody claps for me!"

"If you thought about that, there's no way you could stay angry!" Harmony said.

"**Maybe you're right,**" Broadway replied doubtfully.

"I also have one more solution you can try," Harmony said. "Instead of trying to hold your temper in, you could use it to do something creative!"

"I've heard of losing your temper, but I've never heard of using your temper," Broadway said. "How can I do that?"

"Sometimes," Harmony said, "I dance to music! Or, I'll take out my banjo and make up a song."

"I'm not very good at dancing or singing," Broadway said. "Could I write a story or a play instead?"

"**Good thinking!**" Harmony exclaimed. "You could write your feelings down, or you could draw a picture about them."

"Maybe I'll write my next big hit!" Broadway said. "Thanks for helping me, Harmony. I should go apologize to Bun."

As Broadway waited in line to apologize, he began to feel frustrated. "One, two, three, four..." he whispered to himself. As he counted, the line moved along. Soon, it was his turn to talk to Bun.

"I'm so sorry for losing my temper with you," Broadway told Bun. "It was not fair to treat you that way. From now on, I'll try to be a little more patient and kind. Can we still be friends?"

"**Friends,**" Bun replied, and he shook Broadway's hand.
"Good!" Broadway said. "Because the next time I have a new play opening, there will be a front row ticket waiting for you!"
From that day on, Broadway always tried to control his temper. He counted, he hummed songs, he thought of funny things...

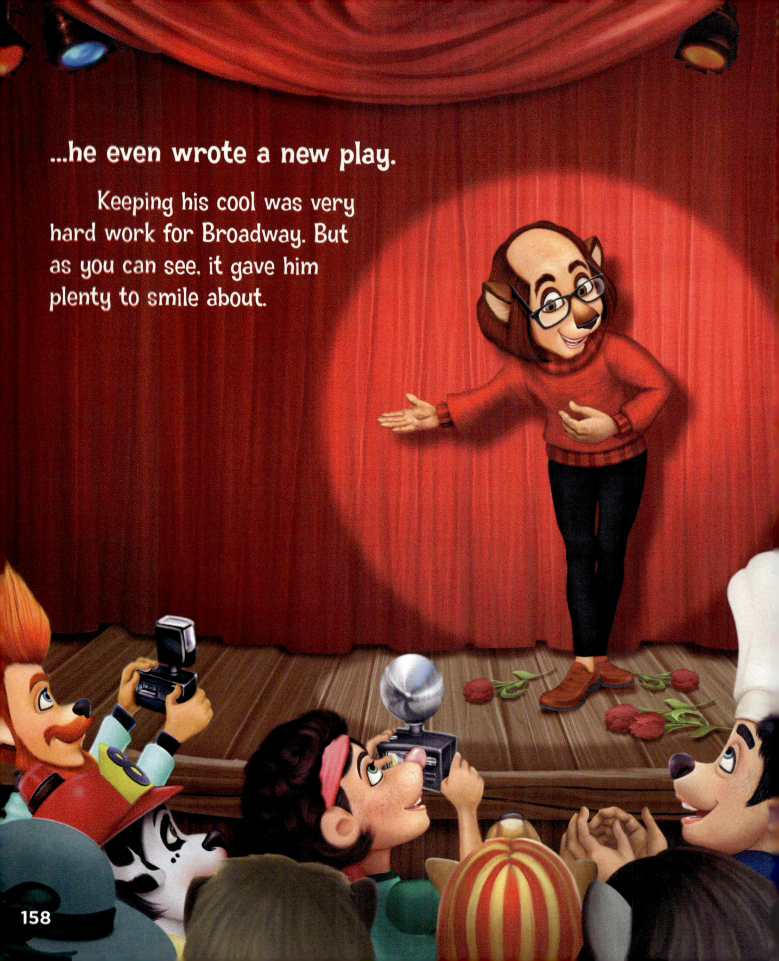

...he even wrote a new play.

Keeping his cool was very hard work for Broadway. But as you can see, it gave him plenty to smile about.

DISCUSSION QUESTIONS

Have you ever felt frustrated? What made you feel that way? How did you handle it?

Can you think of any more ways to deal with being in a bad mood?

KEEPING YOUR COOL

Revised edition. First printing, January 2010.
Copyright 2020 © Lincoln Learning Solutions. All rights reserved.
294 Massachusetts Avenue
Rochester, PA 15074
Visit us on the web at http://www.lincolnlearningsolutions.org.
Midlandia® is a registered trademark of Lincoln Learning Solutions.

Edited by Ashley Mortimer
Character design by Evette Gabriel
Environmental design by Joshua Perry

Nothing But the Truth
A Tales of Midlandia Storybook

by Michael Scotto
illustrated by The Ink Circle

Nothing But the Truth

by Michael Scotto
illustrated by The Ink Circle

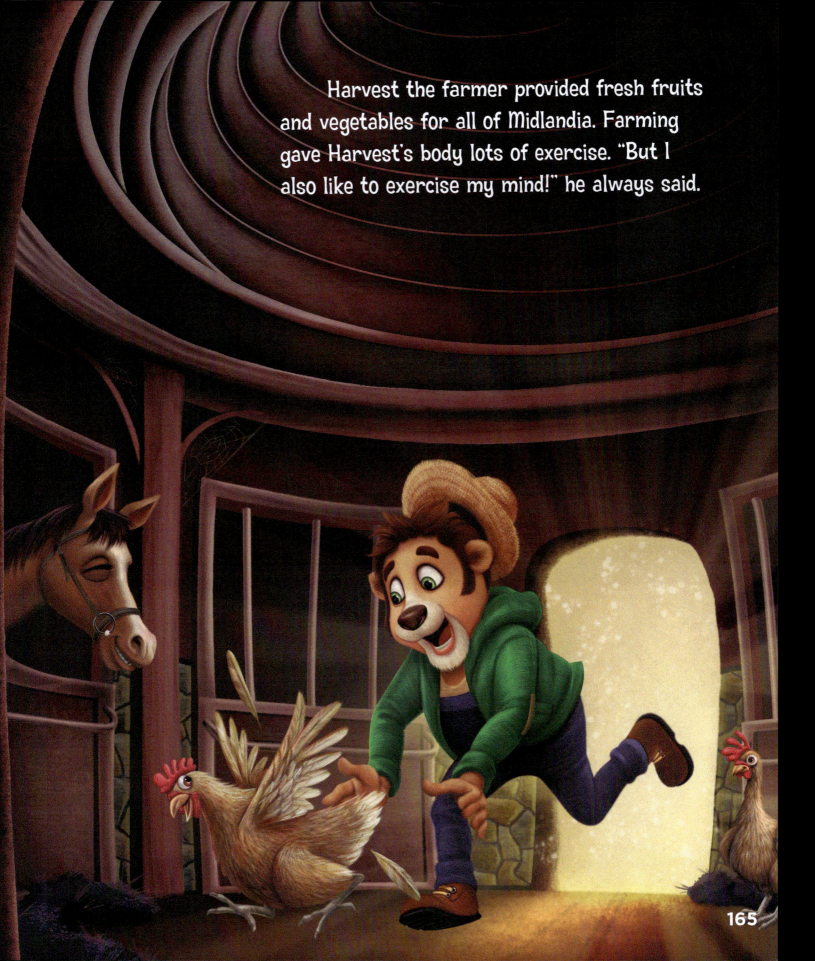

Harvest the farmer provided fresh fruits and vegetables for all of Midlandia. Farming gave Harvest's body lots of exercise. "But I also like to exercise my mind!" he always said.

That is why Harvest loved Vincent's art shows. Vincent was a wonderful artist. Harvest enjoyed looking at Vincent's work and thinking about it.

"**Wow!**" said Harvest as he reached the gallery. "It looks like the whole town showed up!"

Vincent led Harvest and the other guests on a tour of the gallery.

This is amazing! thought Harvest. I like each piece of art better than the last.

After some time, Vincent stopped the tour. "We will take a short break now to enjoy some cookies and music," he announced. "Afterward, I will take everyone around the corner to the back of the gallery. There, I will unveil my masterpiece!" **That sounded very exciting** to Harvest! He did not think he could wait.

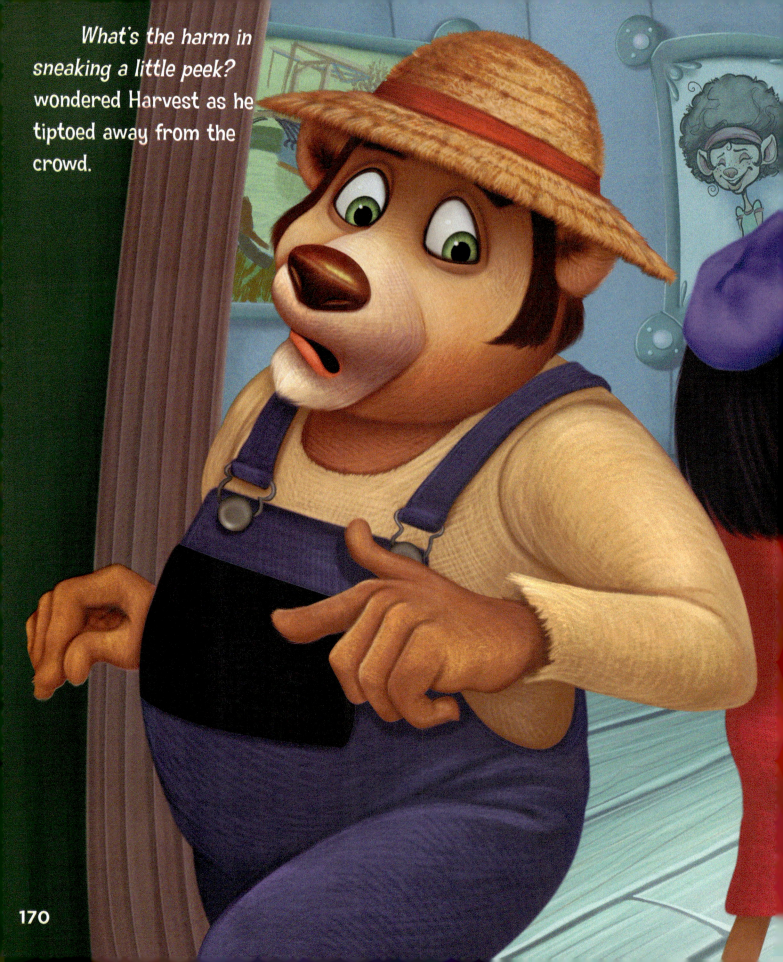

What's the harm in sneaking a little peek? wondered Harvest as he tiptoed away from the crowd.

"Where are you off to?" Vincent called after him. He'd been spotted!

"Umm..." stammered Harvest. "I'm just going to wash my hands."

"Very well," replied Vincent. "You should always wash up before you eat."

Harvest could not believe what he had done! He had never told a fib before. "But it is only because I like Vincent's art so much," he assured himself.

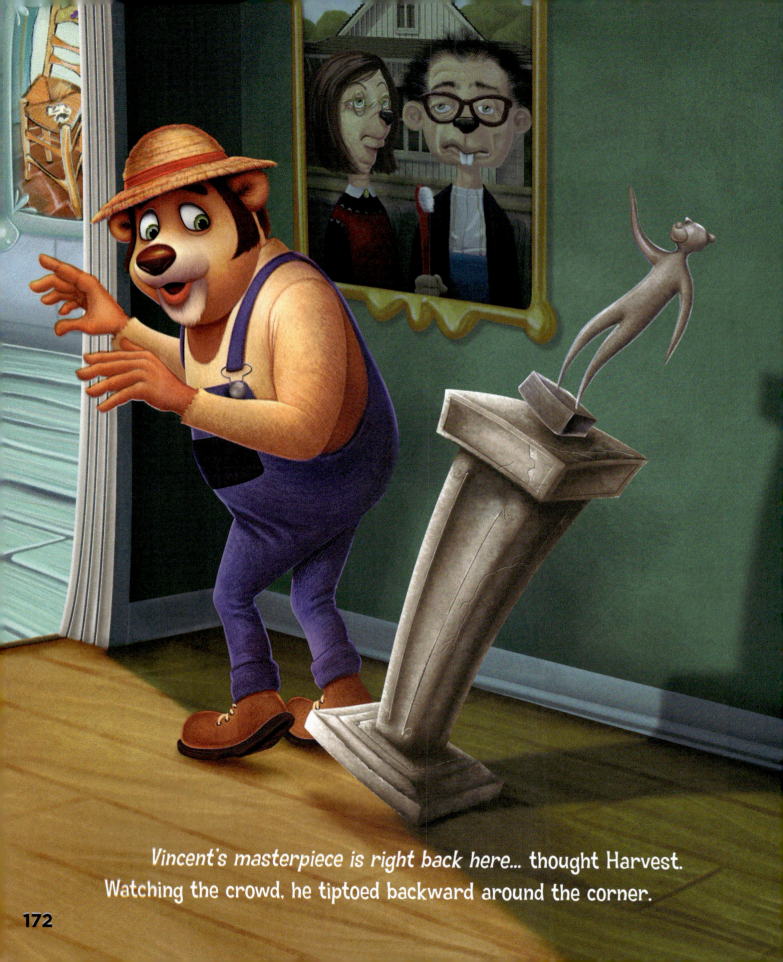

Vincent's masterpiece is right back here... thought Harvest. Watching the crowd, he tiptoed backward around the corner.

Crash!
"**Oh, no!**" cried Harvest. He had bumped into a sculpture and knocked it to the floor.
"**I've ruined Vincent's masterpiece!**"

No one out front had heard the crash. "But they'll find out soon enough," sighed Harvest. "I wasn't even supposed to be back here. How can I face Vincent now?"

"**You don't have to,**" said a voice. Harvest turned in surprise. It was one of those sneaky Inks!

"You don't have to tell Vincent." said the Ink.

"What do you mean?" asked Harvest.

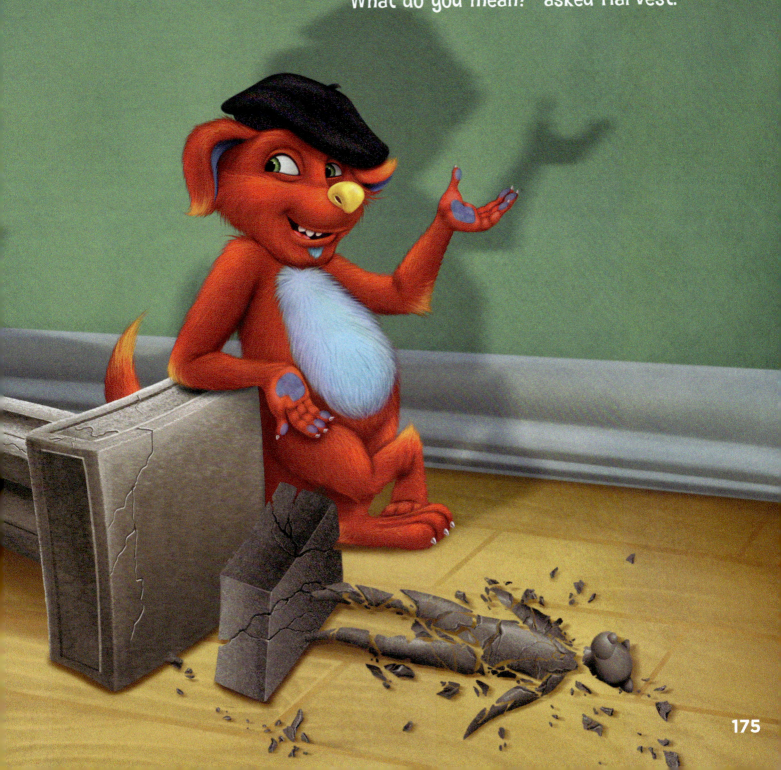

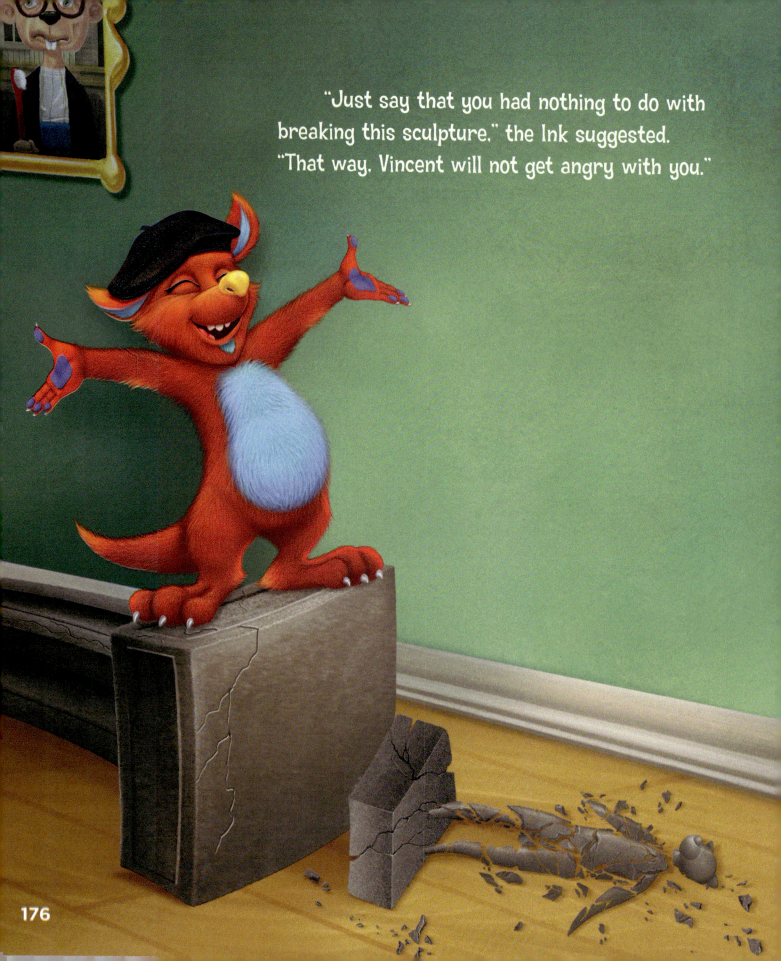

"Just say that you had nothing to do with breaking this sculpture," the Ink suggested. "That way, Vincent will not get angry with you."

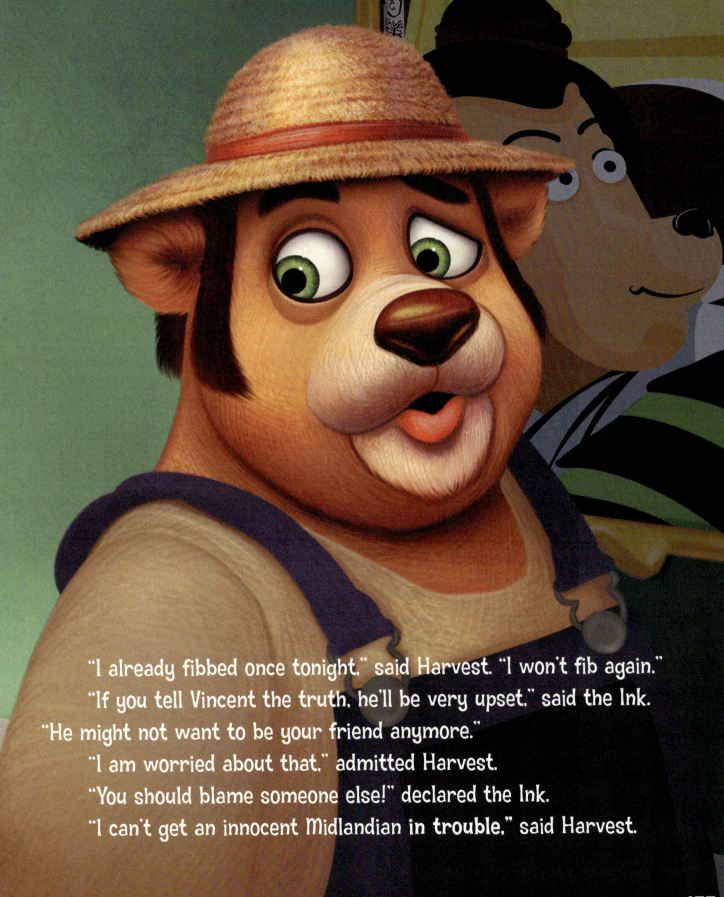

"I already fibbed once tonight," said Harvest. "I won't fib again."

"If you tell Vincent the truth, he'll be very upset," said the Ink. "He might not want to be your friend anymore."

"I am worried about that," admitted Harvest.

"You should blame someone else!" declared the Ink.

"I can't get an innocent Midlandian **in trouble**," said Harvest.

"Then here's what you can tell him!" the Ink exclaimed. "Tell Vincent that you heard a strange noise, so you came to check it out. When you turned the corner, you saw a wild monkey leaping about!"

"He was hungry for bananas, so he climbed the sculpture to look for some. But there were no bananas, so the monkey got angry. You tried to stop that crazy monkey, but it smashed Vincent's masterpiece into masterpieces."

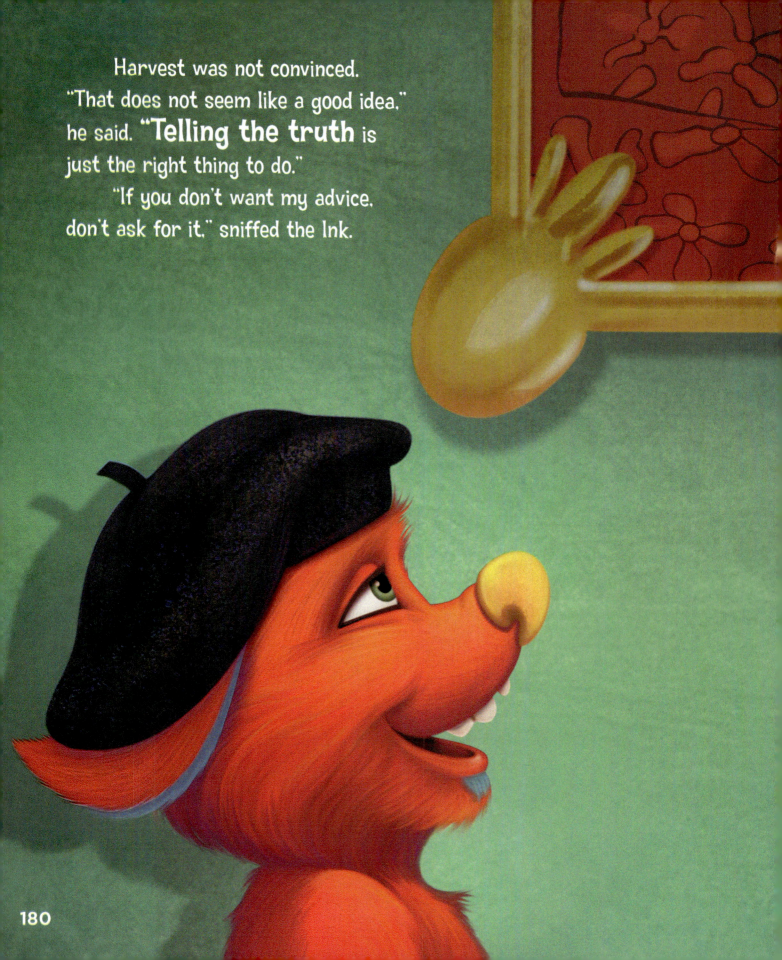

Harvest was not convinced. "That does not seem like a good idea," he said. "**Telling the truth** is just the right thing to do."

"If you don't want my advice, don't ask for it," sniffed the Ink.

"But I didn't ask for your advice!" said Harvest. "What are you doing here anyway?"

The Ink's eyes went wide. "Umm…" he said, looking quite devious. "I'm here because **I love art.**"

Just then, Harvest noticed a second Ink by the wall. "Your friend is trying to rip that painting down!" said Harvest.

"He is not!" insisted the Ink. "He just likes the painting so much that he is giving it a hug."

Harvest spotted a third Ink! "That one's putting Ink prints all over Vincent's work!" cried Harvest.

"He's an art critic."

The music out front stopped. "Inks!" someone cried.

"We've been spotted!" said the Inks. They dashed away just as Vincent and the others hurried in.

"My art," moaned Vincent. "And the Inks destroyed my masterpiece!"

"That's not quite true, Vincent," said Harvest nervously. "The Inks messed up your paintings, but I knocked over your sculpture."

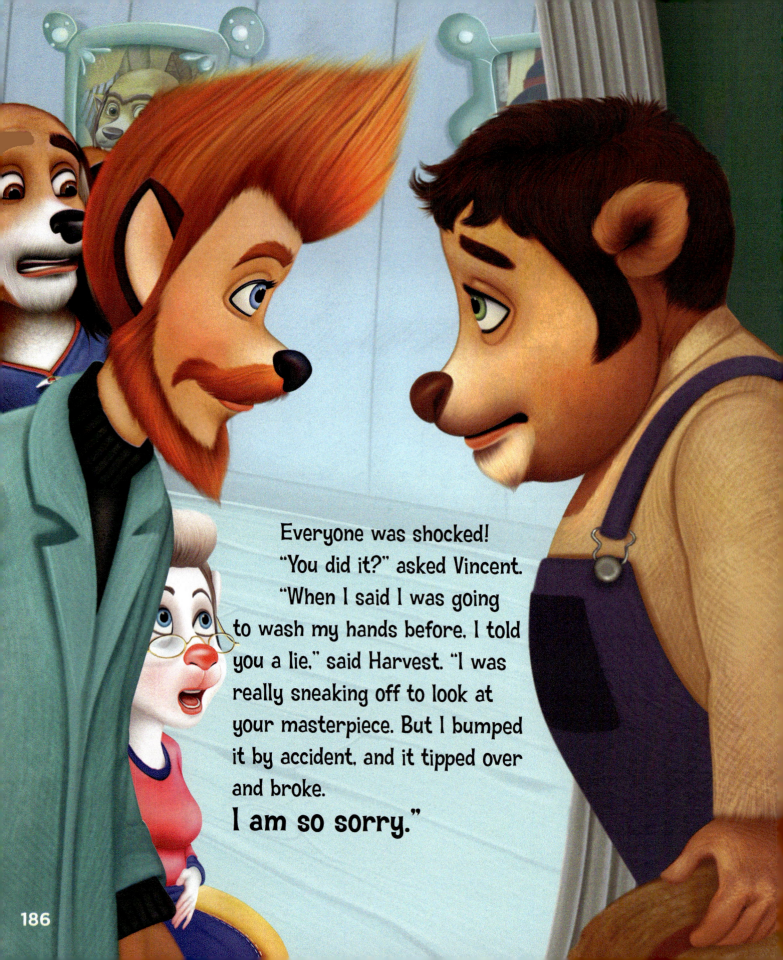

Everyone was shocked! "You did it?" asked Vincent. "When I said I was going to wash my hands before, I told you a lie," said Harvest. "I was really sneaking off to look at your masterpiece. But I bumped it by accident, and it tipped over and broke. **I am so sorry.**"

Vincent did not know what to think. **"This show is over!"** he shouted. "Everyone go home."

The guests all filed out, but Harvest stayed behind. "It's okay if you are angry with me, Vincent," he said. "But I will do anything to make it up to you. I just have to figure out how."

Vincent watched Harvest think. Then, Vincent had a flash of inspiration. "Don't move a muscle!" he said.

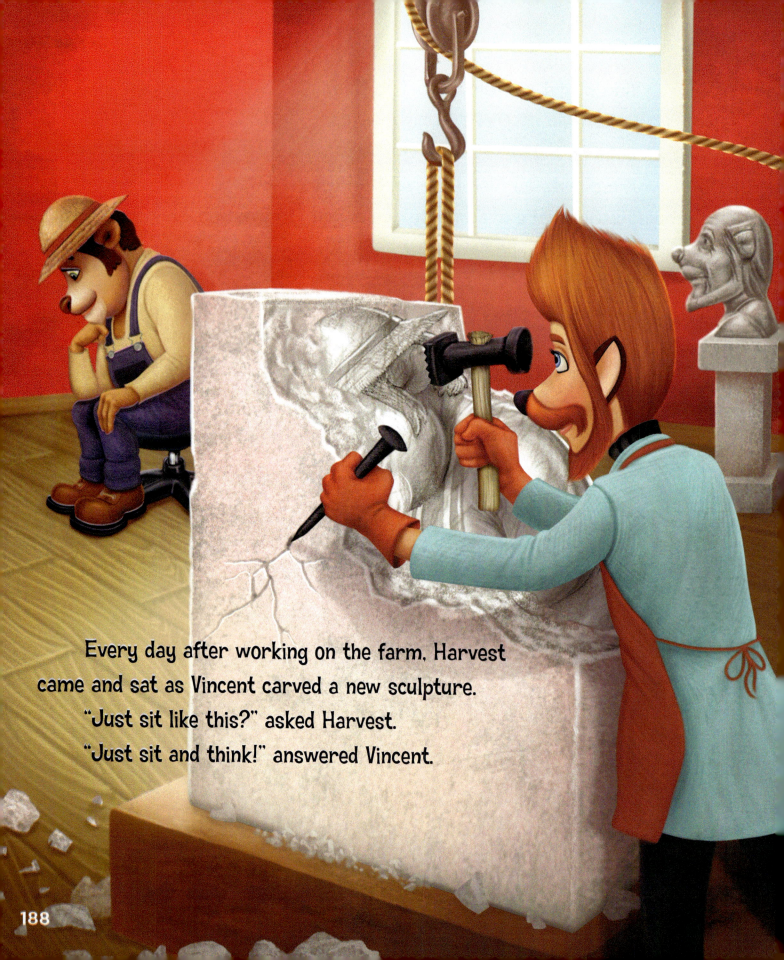

Every day after working on the farm, Harvest came and sat as Vincent carved a new sculpture.

"Just sit like this?" asked Harvest.

"Just sit and think!" answered Vincent.

After some weeks, Vincent was finished.

"This sculpture looks just like me!" cried Harvest.

"I call this piece **The Friend**," said Vincent.

"I don't understand," replied Harvest.

"I was mad when you broke my first sculpture, but you acted bravely by being honest about it," said Vincent. "You could have blamed the Inks, but you took responsibility."

"All I did was tell the truth," said Harvest.

Vincent replied, "That is what a true friend always does."

Discussion Questions

Has anyone ever told you a lie?
How did it make you feel?

What can happen when you do not tell the truth?

NOTHING BUT THE TRUTH

Revised edition. First printing, January 2012.
Copyright 2020 © Lincoln Learning Solutions. All rights reserved.
294 Massachusetts Avenue
Rochester, PA 15074
Visit us on the web at http://www.lincolnlearningsolutions.org.
Midlandia® is a registered trademark of Lincoln Learning Solutions.

Edited by Ashley Mortimer
Midlandian Map by Danielle Caruso
Midlandian Portraits by Danielle Caruso, Doyle Daigle, Matthew Casper, Megan Crow

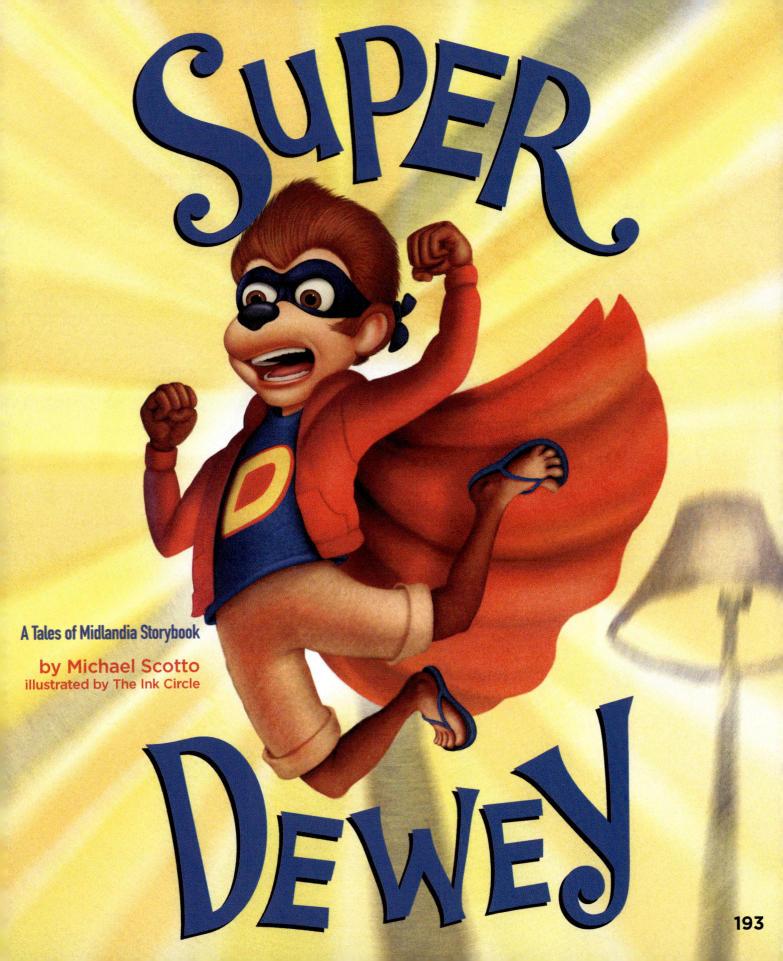

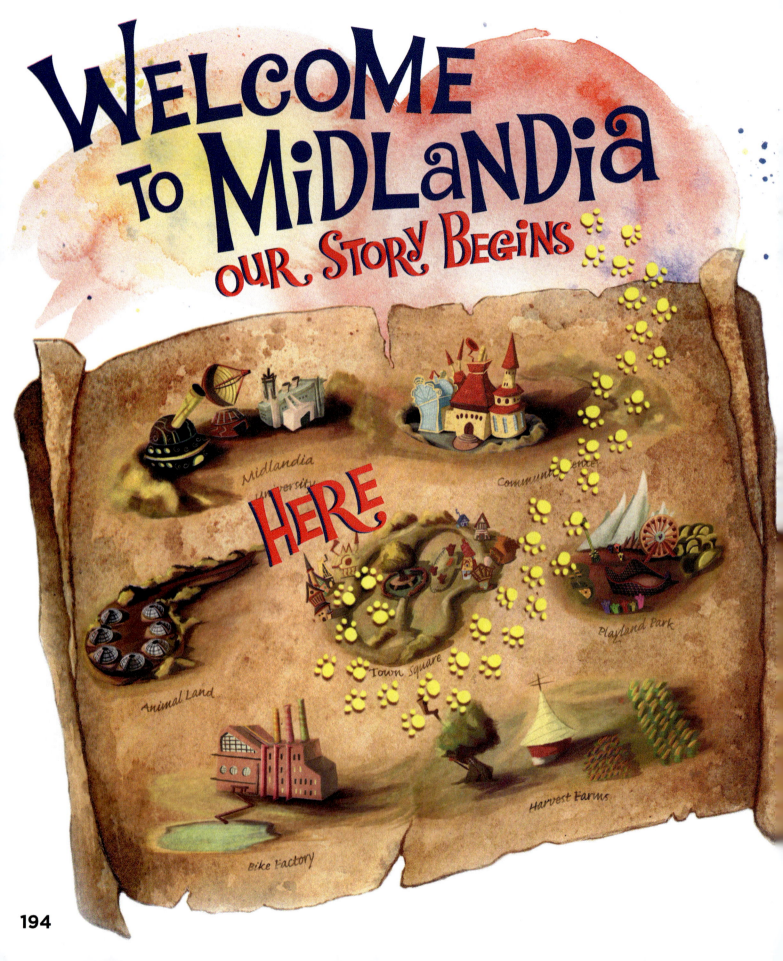

SUPER DEWEY

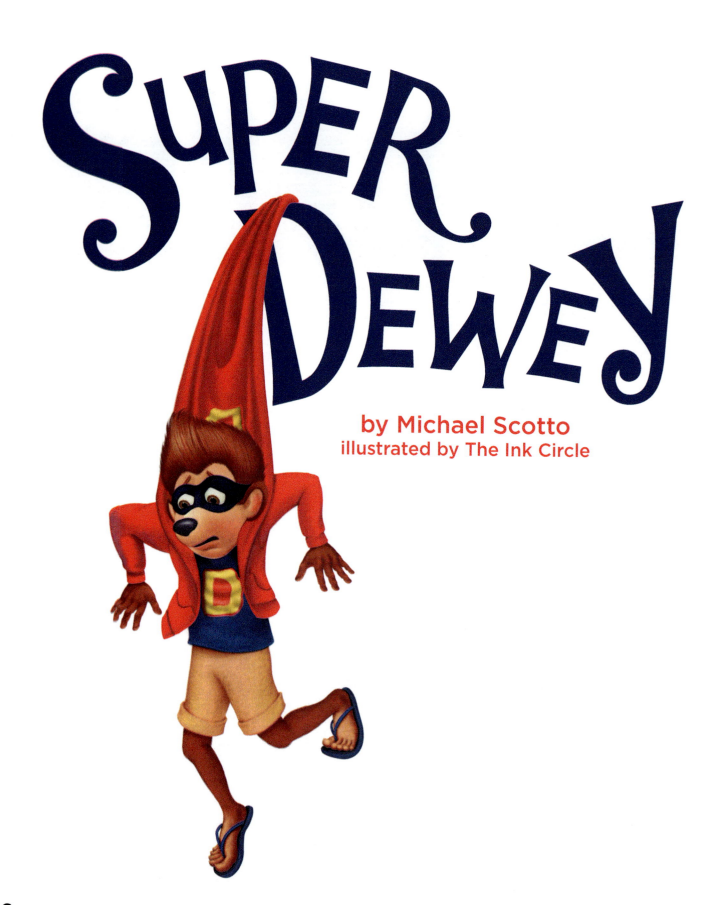

by Michael Scotto
illustrated by The Ink Circle

Dewey was the best librarian in Midlandia.

He knew where every book in the library was supposed to be, and he'd even read most of them.

Comic books were his favorite, though.

While he read, Dewey loved to use his imagination. **I want to be a superhero,** *like in my comic books,* Dewey thought. *That way, I can really make a difference.*

The trouble was that Dewey didn't think he was very super. "How can I be a hero? I don't even have a real cape! I'm just a boring librarian."

Little did Dewey know he was about to get his chance.

One night, after everyone had gone home, some mysterious creatures sneaked into the library and spent the evening causing trouble.

In the morning, Dewey found little paw prints everywhere!

"What a mess! And—oh, no—they mixed up all the books! I'd better get to work."

Around lunchtime, Dewey noticed Star looking through the unorganized stacks of books. "I need your help," Star said. "It's dreadfully important. I have to find this book right away, but it's not on the shelves!"

"Things are a bit of a mess right now," Dewey said. "Come back tomorrow and I'll be sure to have the book waiting for you."

Dewey worked hard all day. "I only have a little left..." he said with a yawn. "I'll take a quick nap, and then...." Dewey dozed off before he could even finish his sentence.

When he opened his eyes, Dewey couldn't believe what he saw. "Oh, no!" he cried. The whole place was wrecked again! *Whoever made this mess must still be here,* Dewey thought. *I'm going to get to the bottom of this.*

Dewey searched through the books and found an encyclopedia of paw prints. He compared the paw prints the troublemakers had left with photographs from the book.

Soon, Dewey found a match!

"I recognize those prints now! This is the work of those pesky little Inks! **But how can I stop them?**"

A trap! he thought.
I'll hide in the shelves so the Inks think that I went home.

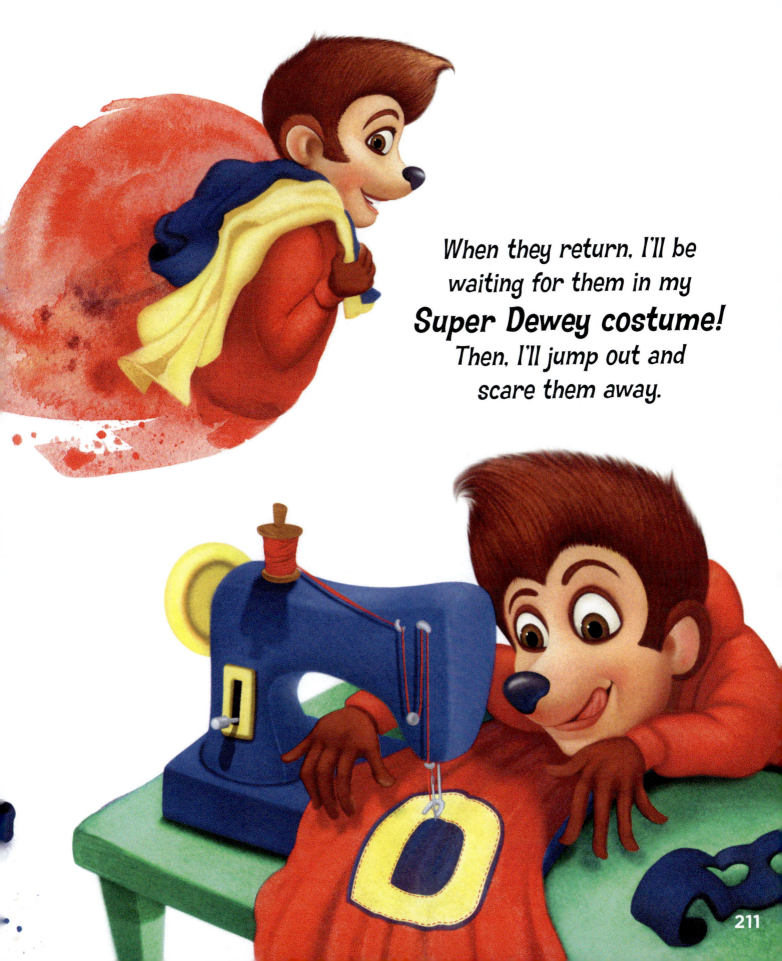

When they return, I'll be waiting for them in my **Super Dewey costume!** Then, I'll jump out and scare them away.

"Okay!" Dewey yelled out to be sure that the Inks heard him. "I guess I'd better go home now!" Dewey shut off the lights, stamped his feet as if he were leaving, and slammed the door.

The Inks whispered to each other as they scampered toward the middle of the floor.

Now's my chance! Dewey thought.

Dewey leapt from the shelf, his cape flapping behind him.

"I've got you!" he yelled out. "Super Dewey to the rescue!"

But before Dewey could capture the Inks, his cape got caught on a lamp! "Help!" he cried, dangling about. The Inks giggled and stuck out their tongues.

Suddenly, there was a knock at the door.

"Dewey, are you in there?" a voice said from outside. "It's Badge! I was just checking out the neighborhood when I heard a ruckus in here."

The Inks scattered back through the hole in the wall.

"I'm over here!" Dewey shouted. "Help me!" Badge helped Dewey down.

"What in the name of Midlandia were you doing?"
"I was just trying to be super," Dewey replied.
"Maybe you should stick to being a librarian," Badge suggested.
"I guess you're right," Dewey said with disappointment.

After Badge left, Dewey examined the library. *What a mess!* he thought. *I wouldn't be a very good librarian if I left it this way. But first....* Dewey covered up the hole where the Inks were getting in, so that they couldn't make any more messes.

By opening time the next morning, Dewey was very tired... but the library was back in perfect order.

Soon, Star came looking for her book. "Hey, Dewey, why the long face?" she asked.

"No reason, I guess," Dewey said glumly. "I found your book for you."

Star jumped up and down with excitement. "Oh, thank you so much, Dewey...**you're my hero!**"

Dewey looked at her, puzzled. "Really?"

"Of course!" Star said. "If you hadn't found this book for me, I would never have been able to get my work done."

Dewey smiled. *Maybe being a librarian isn't so boring after all*, he thought. And from then on, Dewey always remembered that **you don't have to be super to be a hero.**

Discussion Questions

Dewey's story shows us that everyday people can be heroes. Name someone in your life who is a hero to you. Why do you look up to this person?

In the story, Dewey wished he was a superhero with superpowers. If you could be a superhero for a day, what superpower would you choose?

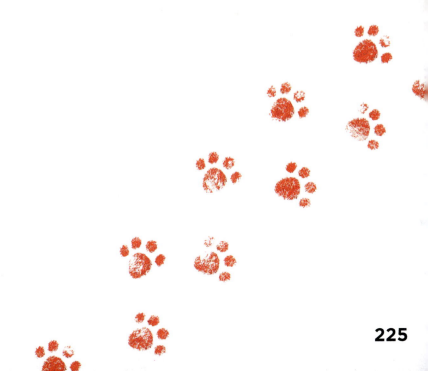

SUPER DEWEY

Revised edition. First printing, January 2008.
Copyright 2020 © Lincoln Learning Solutions. All rights reserved.
294 Massachusetts Avenue
Rochester, PA 15074
Visit us on the web at http://www.lincolnlearningsolutions.org.
Midlandia® is a registered trademark of Lincoln Learning Solutions.

Edited by Ashley Mortimer
Character design by Evette Gabriel
Environmental design by Joshua Perry

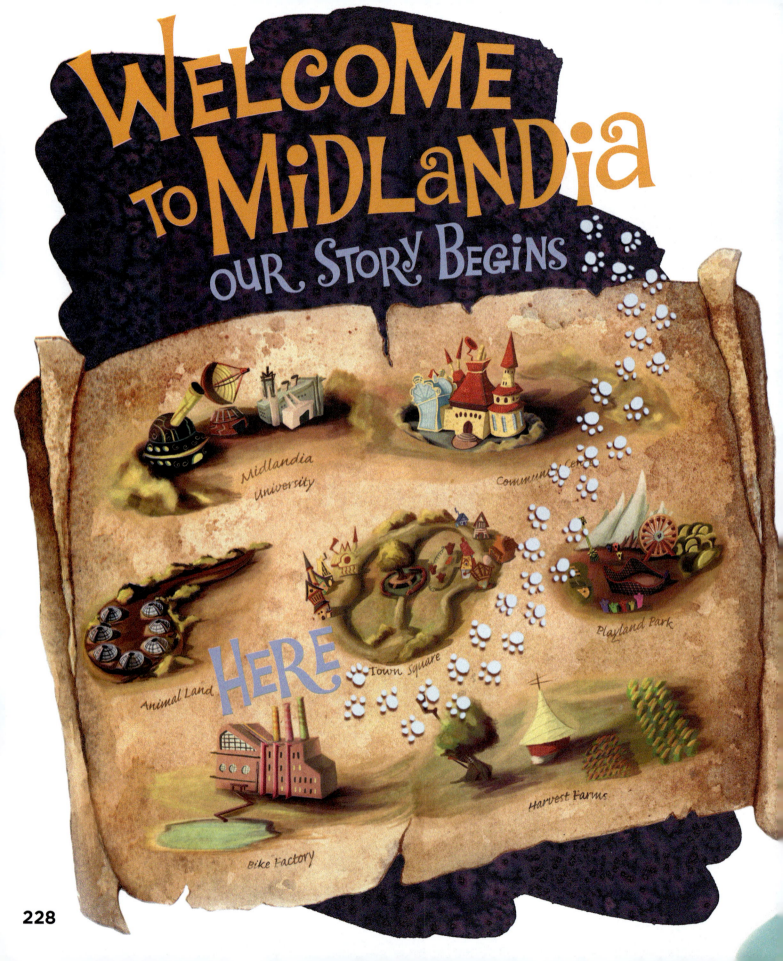

Sweet Tooth Bun

by Michael Scotto
illustrated by The Ink Circle

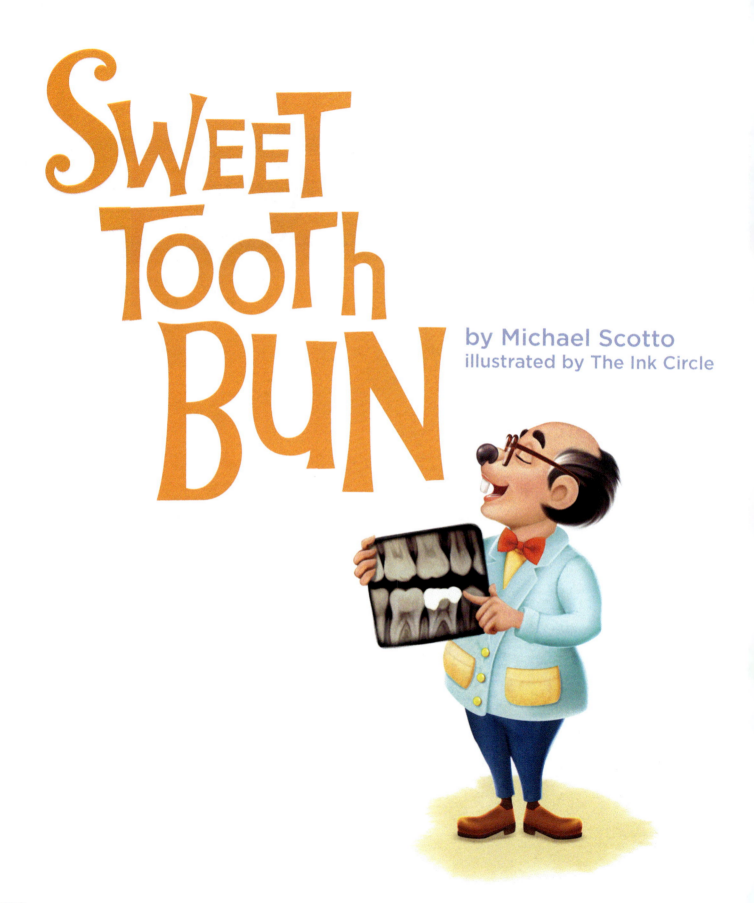

Bun the baker was famous for his sweets. Cakes and pies, cream puffs and cookies—Bun baked them all. If a treat looked less than perfect, Bun would not serve it. He would just eat it himself.

Sometimes, Bun would make a mistake just so he could have a snack.

"Oh, goodness!" Bun said to Antigua. "I dropped your star cookie and it broke into pieces. I can't sell it to you...it's pointless! I'd better just eat it myself."

But when he took a bite of the sweet, crispy cookie, something strange happened.

"Ouch!" Bun cried.

"Are you all right?" asked Antigua.

"No, I certainly am not," Bun replied. "I have a terrible ache in my tooth."

"A toothache?" Antigua replied. "That's the worst! Maybe you should pay a visit to Dr. Brushy."

Bun turned whiter than whipped cream. "You mean...go to the dentist?" he asked.

"**When your teeth hurt,**" Antigua said, "the dentist is the one to see."

"No, no," Bun said. "Remember when I said my toothache was terrible? I was only kidding then. See?" He took another nibble, wincing with each crunch. "**Oww, oww...I mean, yum-yum!**"

Antigua would not be fooled. "Come on, Bun," she said. "I'm taking you to the dentist, and that is final."

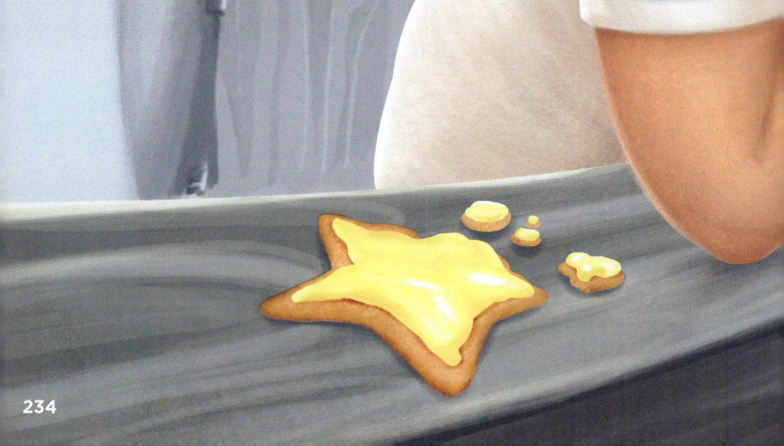

235

Antigua led Bun toward the office that Dr. Brushy shared with his twin sister, Doc Fixit.

"Why are you being so mean?" Bun asked.

"I am being your friend," Antigua replied. "A good friend would never let her best pal suffer."

"You don't want me to suffer, eh?" Bun scoffed. "I know what **nasty** things happen at the dentist!"

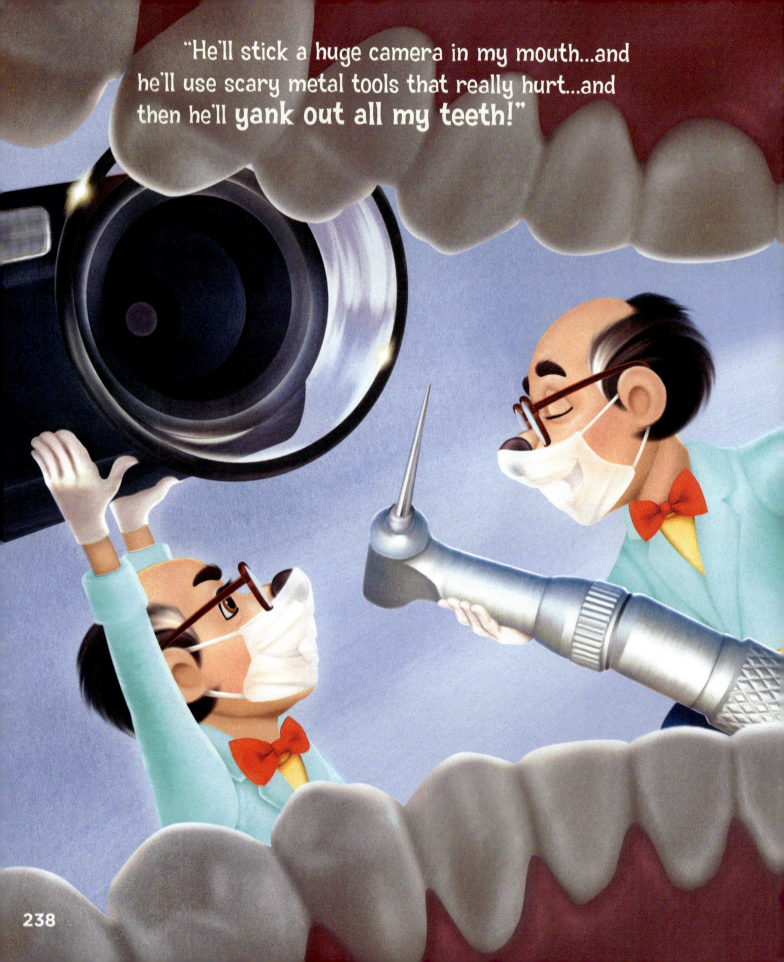

Antigua and Bun reached the door to Dr. Brushy's office.

"I've seen Dr. Brushy many times," Antigua said. "He'll take great care of your smile."

"Fine," Bun huffed. "But when Dr. Brushy steals all my teeth, you'll have to feed me."

Antigua entered the office with Bun. Dr. Brushy greeted them with a friendly wave. "Antigua, my dear!" Dr. Brushy said. "Hi, Dr. Brushy!" Antigua said. "Bun has a toothache. **Can you help him?**"

Bun joined Brushy in the exam room.

"Before we start, Bun, I need you to put on this special vest," Brushy said. "Be careful; it's a little heavy."

"This looks sort of like an apron I'd wear in my bakery," Bun said.

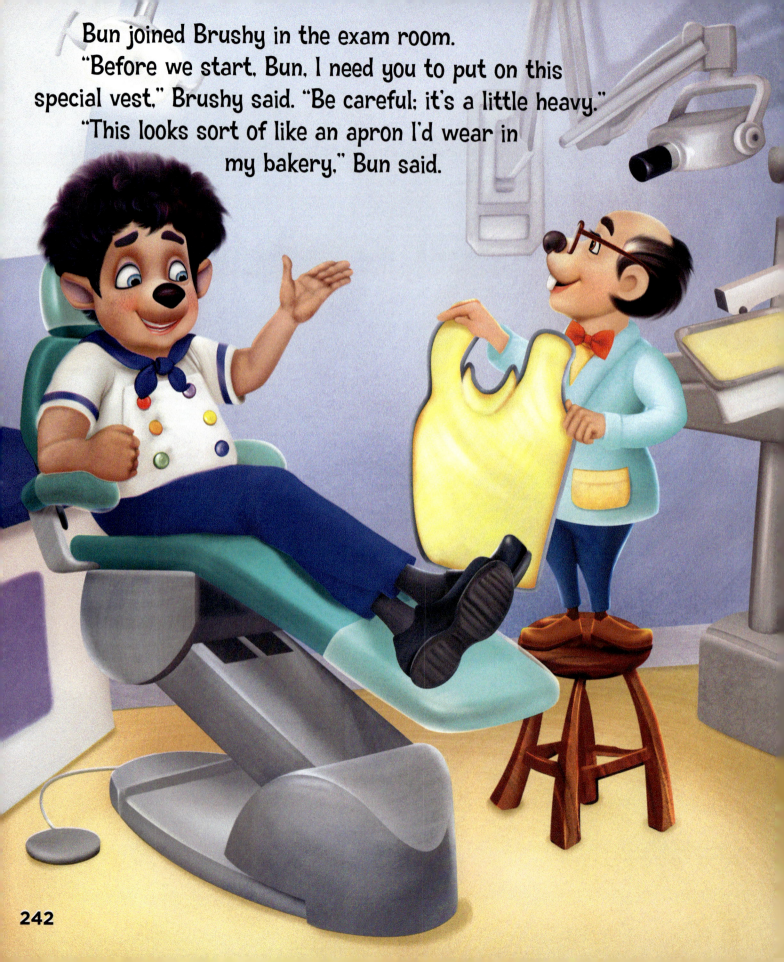

"Please sit very still," Brushy said. "The machine next to you will make some funny noises, but it won't hurt you."

Bun did what Brushy said. Brushy flipped a switch, and the machine began to hum and click for a few seconds.

"Congratulations!" Brushy said. "You've just had your first dental X-ray!"

"What's an X-ray?" Bun asked.

"It's a special picture of your teeth," Brushy told him. "When the picture develops, I can look at it and find the cause of your toothache."

Bun was stunned! "You already took the picture? But I didn't have to open my mouth or anything."

"What did you think I'd do?" Brushy asked with a smile. "Stuff a camera in there?"

Bun turned a little red.

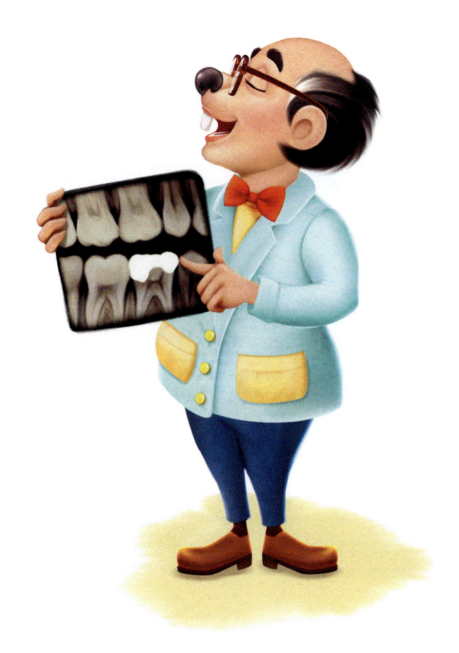

Soon, Bun's X-ray was ready.

"I think I see the trouble, Bun," Brushy said. "Do you see that white spot on your tooth? **That, my friend, is a cavity.**"

"A cavity!" Bun howled. "That's horrible! Right?"

"Well, a cavity is not good news," Brushy began. "But it is a very common problem. A cavity is a weak spot or hole on the outside of your tooth. Luckily, I know just how to deal with it."

"I knew it," Bun sighed. "You're going to yank out my teeth. **Goodbye, crispy cookies; hello, mushy cereal.**"

"Oh, no, I won't have to pull out any of your teeth," Brushy said. "That does happen sometimes, but only in real emergencies. Dentists always do their best to help your teeth so they do not have to be removed. All we need to do is clean out the cavity."

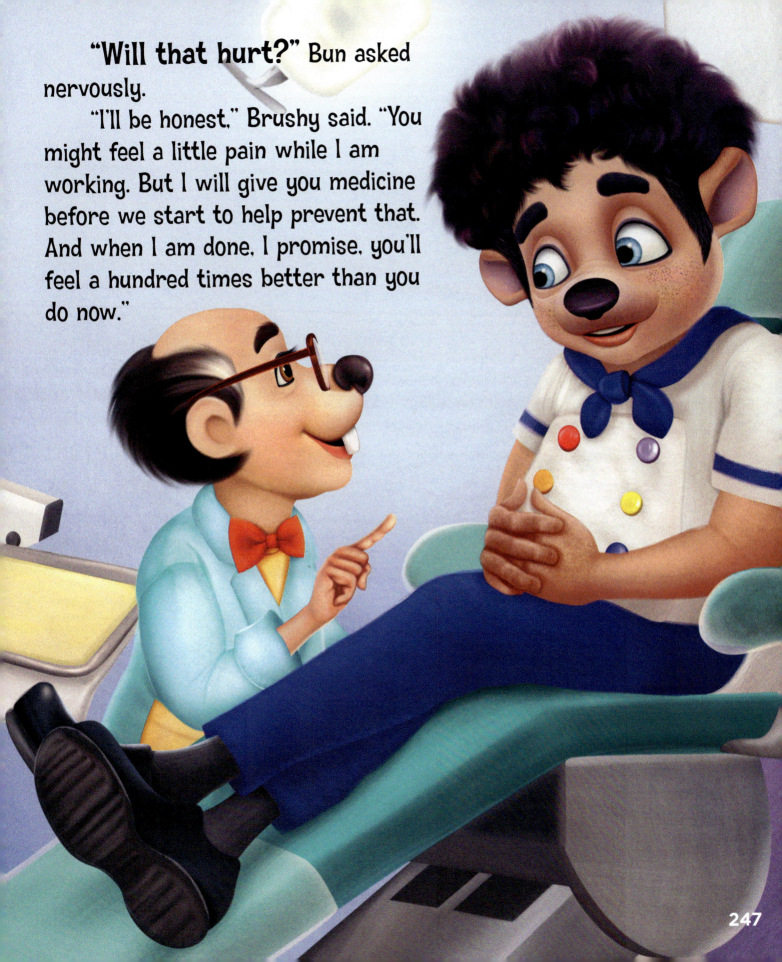

"Will that hurt?" Bun asked nervously.

"I'll be honest," Brushy said. "You might feel a little pain while I am working. But I will give you medicine before we start to help prevent that. And when I am done, I promise, you'll feel a hundred times better than you do now."

Bun decided to trust Brushy. Before they got to work, Brushy showed Bun all of his tools. That way, Bun would not be scared or surprised.

"**I'm ready,**" Bun said.

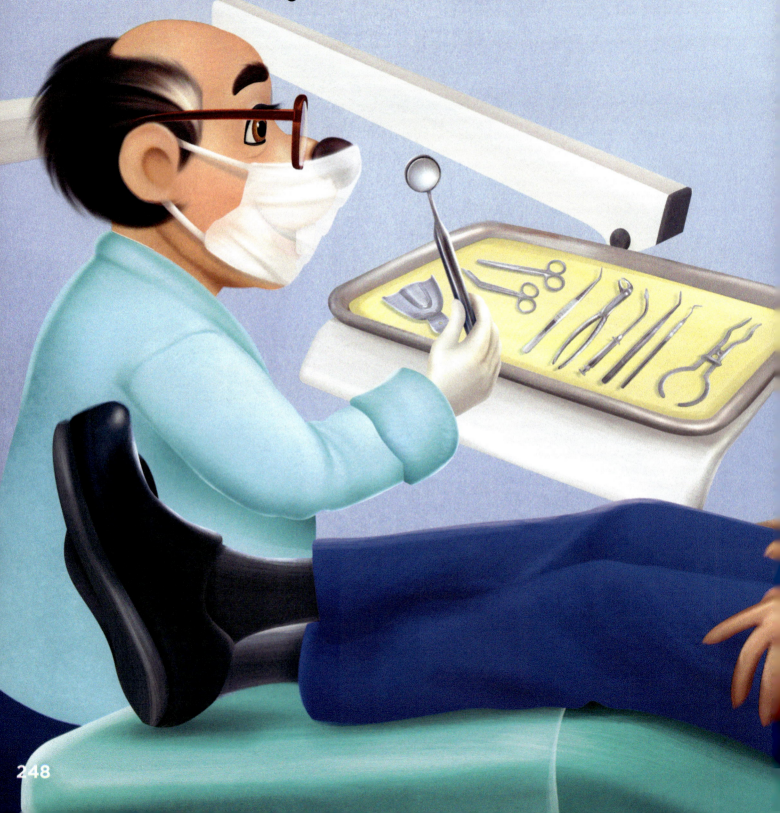

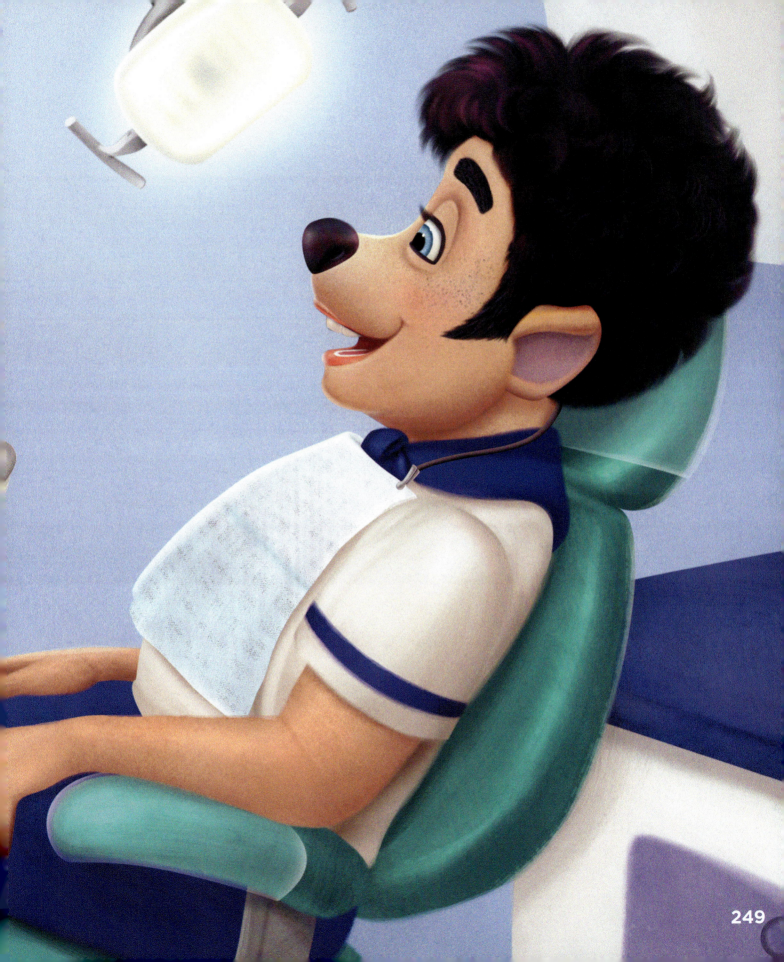

Before long, Bun was good as new. "I feel so much better!" he told Antigua in the waiting room. "I should have listened to you all along. **Thanks for being such a good friend.**"

"You took great care of me, Dr. Brushy...but I don't want any more cavities," Bun said. "How can I keep them away?"

"One key to a healthy smile is to **brush** your teeth and **floss** twice every day," Brushy said.

"There's also something else," Brushy added. "I know you have a sweet tooth, Bun. But the germs that cause cavities love sugar. If you cut back on sugar, that can help fight cavities."

"No more sweets?" Bun said. "Antigua, this guy is bananas!"

"**I didn't say 'no more sweets,'**" Brushy said. "Even I like a piece of pie now and then. But, it is not good for your teeth to eat cupcakes and cookies all day long. Perhaps you could try something new." Brushy pointed to a plate on the table. "Have a fresh carrot stick. I keep a special stash in case I get hungry at work."

Bun held up the carrot and smirked. "There's no frosting or anything," he said. But then he took a bite… and his eyes grew wide. **"Holy plum pudding!"** Bun said. "It's crunchy and juicy, and it's a little sweet, too!"

"You see?" Brushy said. "Lots of healthful foods taste great—without dumping sugar all over them."

Back at the bakery, Bun began to experiment with new, more healthful foods. Soon, he was famous for more than his sweets. Midlandians loved his salads, his toasted apple slices, and even his peanut butter crackers! Bun still ate cookies sometimes, but he was happy to have so many more choices. And as he told his customers, "My teeth are a lot happier, too!"

DISCUSSION QUESTIONS

Have you ever been to the dentist?
Why did you go?
How was your visit?

Pretend that you have a friend who is afraid of going to the dentist. How would you help your friend?

SWEET TOOTH BUN

Revised edition. First printing, January 2009.
Copyright 2020 © Lincoln Learning Solutions. All rights reserved.
294 Massachusetts Avenue
Rochester, PA 15074
Visit us on the web at http://www.lincolnlearningsolutions.org.
Midlandia® is a registered trademark of Lincoln Learning Solutions.

Edited by Ashley Mortimer
Character design by Evette Gabriel
Environmental design by Joshua Perry

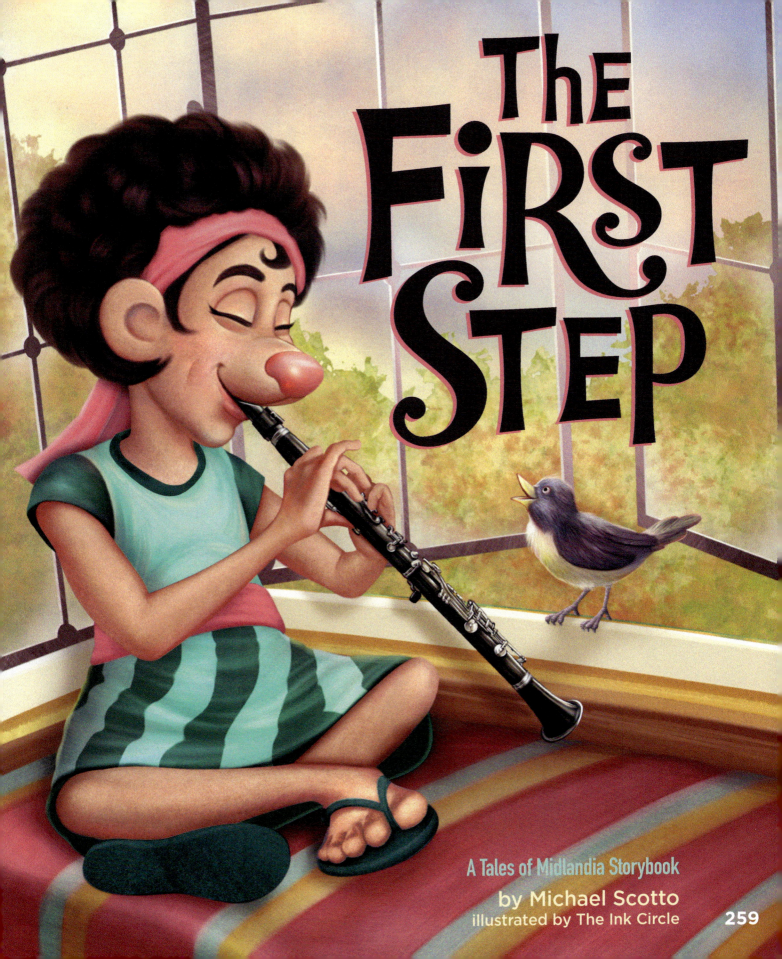

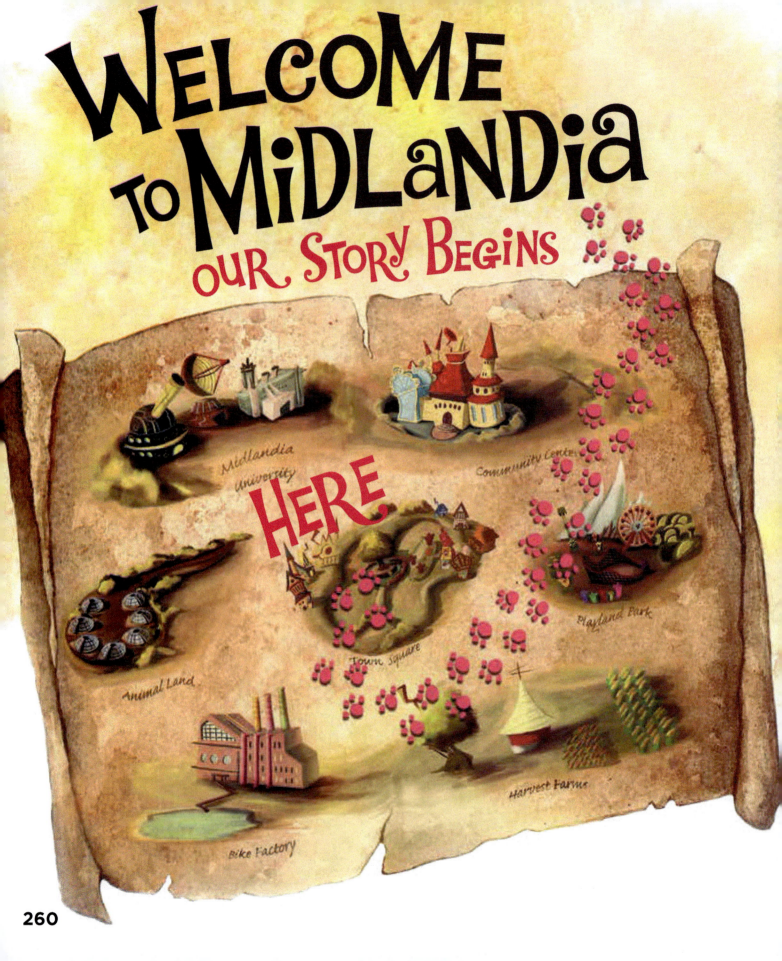

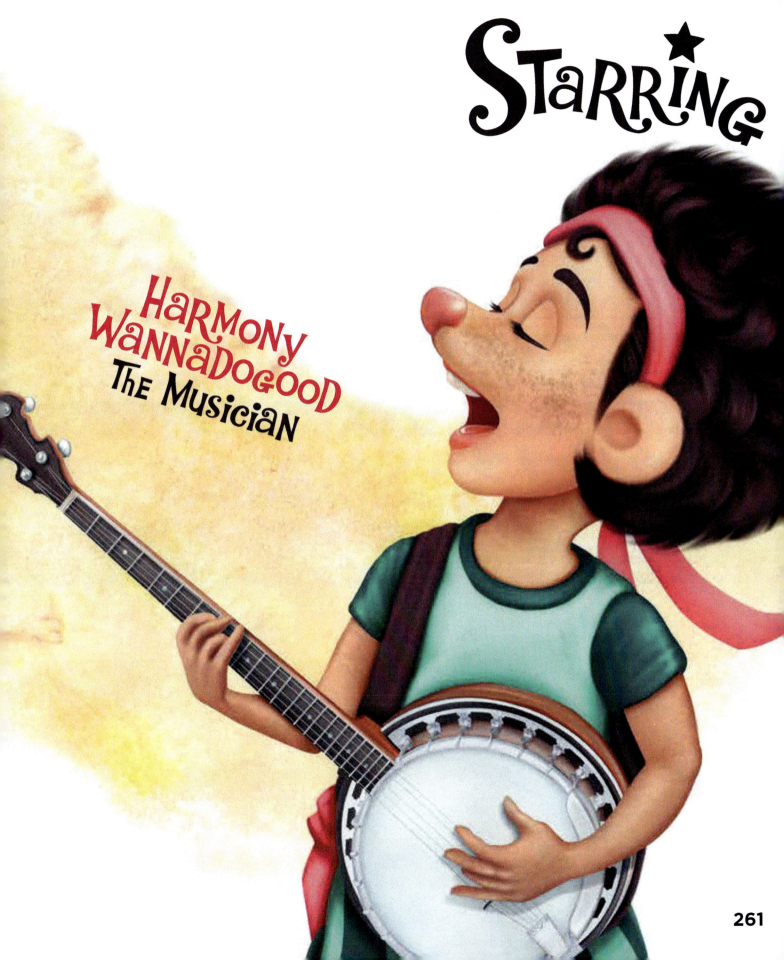

The First Step

by Michael Scotto
illustrated by The Ink Circle

Monday, Tuesday, Wednesday, Thursday, and Friday; everyone in Midlandia worked hard all week.

But on the weekend, it was playtime! Midlandians played their favorite games and hobbies in the Town Square and beyond.

There was one Midlandian, though—a very bright and brave young lady—who wanted to try something new.

Harmony was a musician. She could play the drums and the banjo, the flute and the trombone. Today, she was in the mood to try a new instrument.

"I'm going to learn the clarinet!" she declared.

Harmony sat outside to practice. She imagined the beautiful songs she would play. I'll sound prettier than a bird, she thought. When she blew her first note, though...

...Harmony did not sound as pretty as a bird. She did not even sound as good as a duck or goose. "I sound like a screaming monkey!" she cried. She took a deep breath and gave the clarinet another try. Instead of notes, all Harmony got were squeaks, squawks, screeches, and squeals. Others began to notice.

"What is that terrible noise?" one Midlandian asked another.

Soon, Chief Tatupu rushed around the corner where Harmony was playing. Chief was the leader of Midlandia. He was a great helper and friend.

"What is happening?" asked Chief. "I heard the most awful cries of pain!"

"Those weren't awful cries of pain!" Harmony moaned. "They were the awful cries of my clarinet."

Chief was very embarrassed. "Oh, I am sorry," he said. "I did not realize."

"I'm terrible at playing this thing," Harmony grumbled. **"I quit!"**

Chief knelt down beside Harmony. "You must not quit so soon," he said.

"Why not?" asked Harmony. "You said it yourself. I sound worse than a bicycle crash."

"I did not quite say that," Chief replied with a smile. "If you want to know the truth, what you sounded like was the first time Builda played tennis."

Harmony was puzzled. "That doesn't make any sense," she said. "Builda is a great athlete, and tennis is her favorite hobby."

"She is very good at tennis now," replied Chief. "But the first time Builda ever tried to play...

Harmony was surprised. "You mean Builda wasn't always good at tennis?" she asked.

"Almost no one does an activity very well the first time they try it," Chief said. He pointed around the Town Square. "Look around. I bet that I could tell you a story about every single Midlandian out here."

Chief pointed at Doc Fixit. "Doc Fixit is the best doctor around," he said. "But the first time she put on someone's cast...

"...she ended up in a very sticky situation."

"There is Sew, the seamstress," Chief noted. "She makes terrific dresses. But on her first try...

Chief spotted Bun, the town baker. "Bun makes delicious muffins every day," he told Harmony. "But I remember his first batch...

"...left him quite battered."

"Posta delivers mail all around town on her bike," Chief said. "But the first time she tried to ride…

Chief began to laugh. "And you should have seen me the first time I fished," he said. "On my first boat ride…

"Even you had a hard time with something new?" asked Harmony in amazement.

"Everyone does," Chief replied. "Trying a new thing is like walking on a long and bumpy journey. The first step is always the toughest one to take. You might be scared. You might even stumble. But without that first step, you can never go anywhere."

Harmony finally smiled. "You're right," she said. "I should get back to practicing. But maybe I'll take it inside until I get a little better."

"Good luck!" Chief said.

Squeaking and squawking away, Harmony practiced her clarinet. It would be a long time until she sounded as pretty as a bird. But Harmony knew that each new day she practiced would bring her one step closer.

Discussion Questions

Can you think of a new thing that you have tried recently? Did you have fun? Do you think that you will try it again?

Harmony had a tough time playing the clarinet. If you were Harmony's friend, what would you tell her to make her feel better?

THE FIRST STEP

Revised edition. First printing, January 2010.
Copyright 2020 © Lincoln Learning Solutions. All rights reserved.
294 Massachusetts Avenue
Rochester, PA 15074
Visit us on the web at http://www.lincolnlearningsolutions.org.
Midlandia® is a registered trademark of Lincoln Learning Solutions.

Edited by Ashley Mortimer
Character design by Evette Gabriel
Environmental design by Joshua Perry

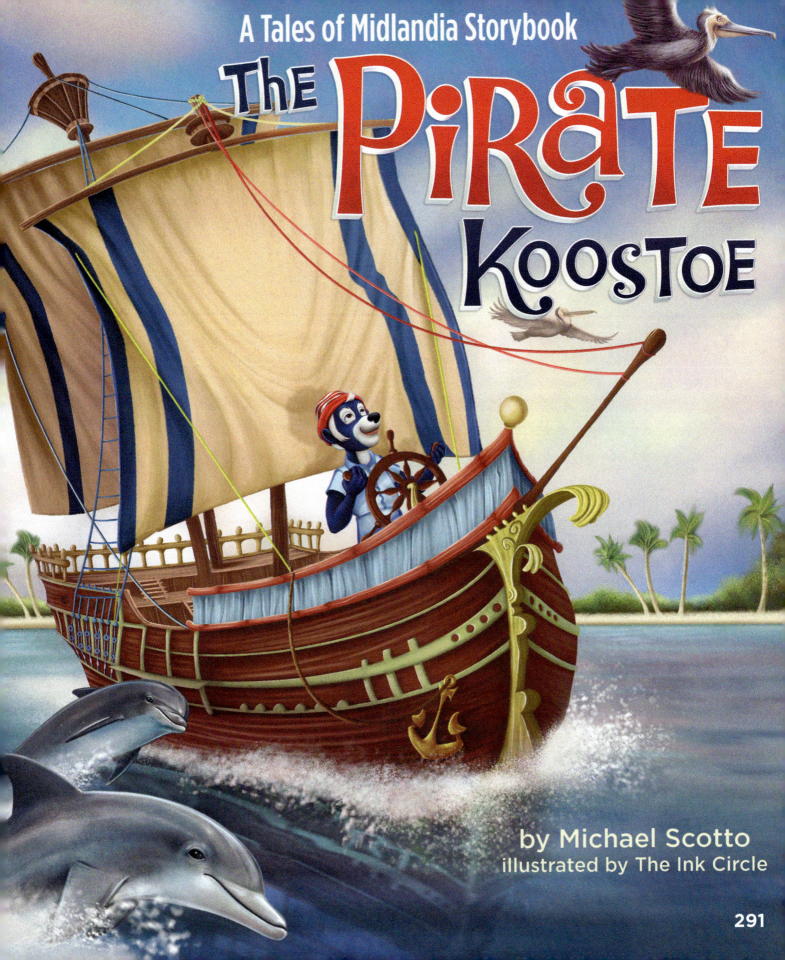

The Pirate Koostoe

by Michael Scotto
illustrated by The Ink Circle

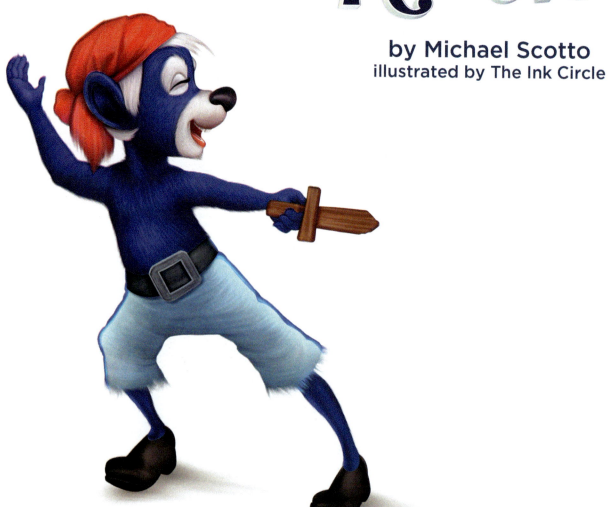

Koostoe O. Bobo had a fascinating job. He was a ship captain. He loved to explore the open sea.

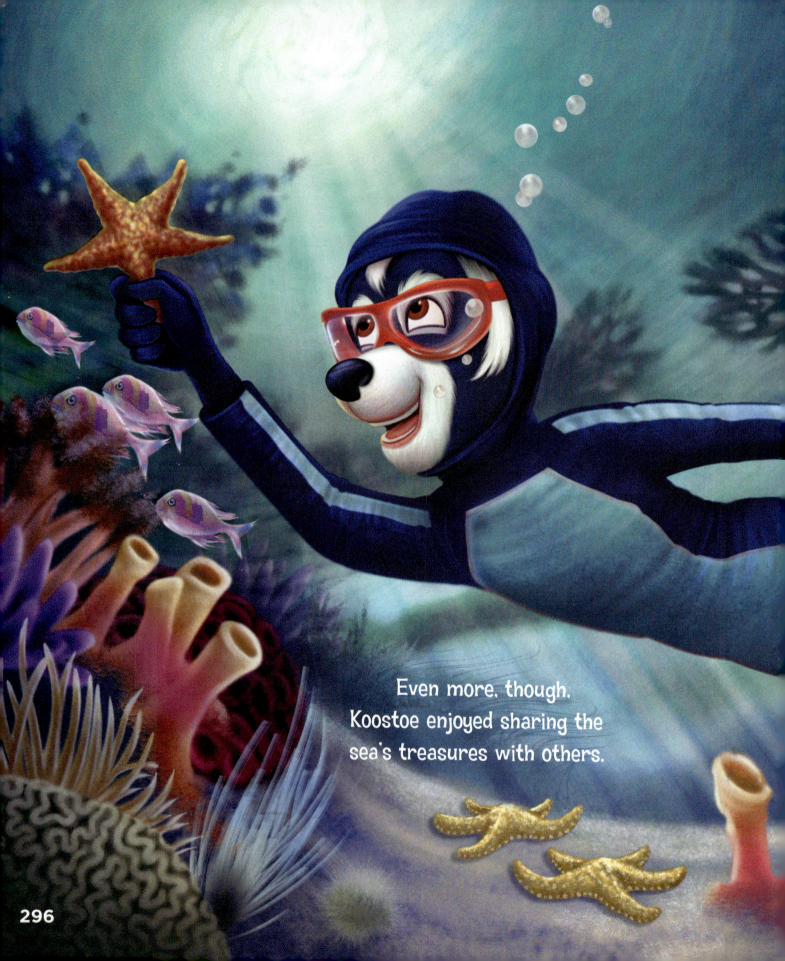

Even more, though, Koostoe enjoyed sharing the sea's treasures with others.

"**A starfish!**" Koostoe bubbled. "He would be a perfect fit for Wilda's saltwater aquarium at the zoo."

Koostoe had not always thought this way, however. He had always loved the sea. And yes, he had always loved treasure. But he had not always cared about sharing. In fact, when Koostoe was a boy....

"**I want to be a pirate!**" cried young Koostoe. He and some other Midlandians had been sharing what they wanted to be when they grew up.

"A pirate?" Nueva asked curiously. "What do pirates do?"

"Whatever they want!" declared Koostoe. "Pirates get to sail on the ocean all day long. But the best part about being a pirate is that it's your job to search for treasure!"

"That sounds perfect." said Buck.

"I'm not so sure being a pirate is a good idea," said Dewey.

"Oh, really?" replied Koostoe with a smirk.

"I've read about pirates at the library," said Dewey. "They are not very nice. They get their treasure by taking it from others."

"That sounds like stealing to me," observed Nueva.

Koostoe grew upset. "It's not stealing when you're a pirate!" he shouted. "You're just jealous because I found the perfect job! And I'm going to start working today. From now on, you will call me...**the pirate Koostoe!**"

Since he did not have a ship, Koostoe first tried to be a pirate on land. "Arrr!" he would growl, waving his little wooden sword. "I am the pirate Koostoe! Surrender your treasure!"

But nobody found him to be very convincing.

"What a darling costume!" raved Sew the seamstress.

"Your voice sounds funny," noted Doc Fixit. "Are you getting a cold?"

Koostoe began to grow sad, and a little angry, too. "All I want is to get some treasure," he sighed. But then, Koostoe had an idea.

"A ship!" he exclaimed. "That's my trouble. To be a real pirate, I need a ship. **And I know just the one...."**

Every weekend, Chief Tatupu took his boat out to go fishing. Chief worked hard as the leader of Midlandia, and fishing helped him to relax.

Such a perfectly peaceful day, Chief thought as he rowed.

Behind Chief, Koostoe sneaked up quietly on his little raft. As he paddled, though, the young pirate began to have doubts. *Maybe Nueva and Dewey were right,* he thought. *This feels like stealing,* and **stealing is wrong.**

But then, Koostoe spotted something next to Chief in the boat. It was a wooden box with golden edges.

"Treasure!" cried Koostoe, and when he drew very close...

Koostoe jumped up and shouted, "Hold it right there, Chief! I claim that treasure chest for the pirate Koostoe. Hand it over or walk the plank!"

Chief saw the young Midlandian and chuckled. "Do you mean my tackle box?" he asked. "This is where I keep my hooks and bait. I am afraid that you cannot borrow it today."

"That's where you're wrong, matey!" growled Koostoe. **"Arrr!"**

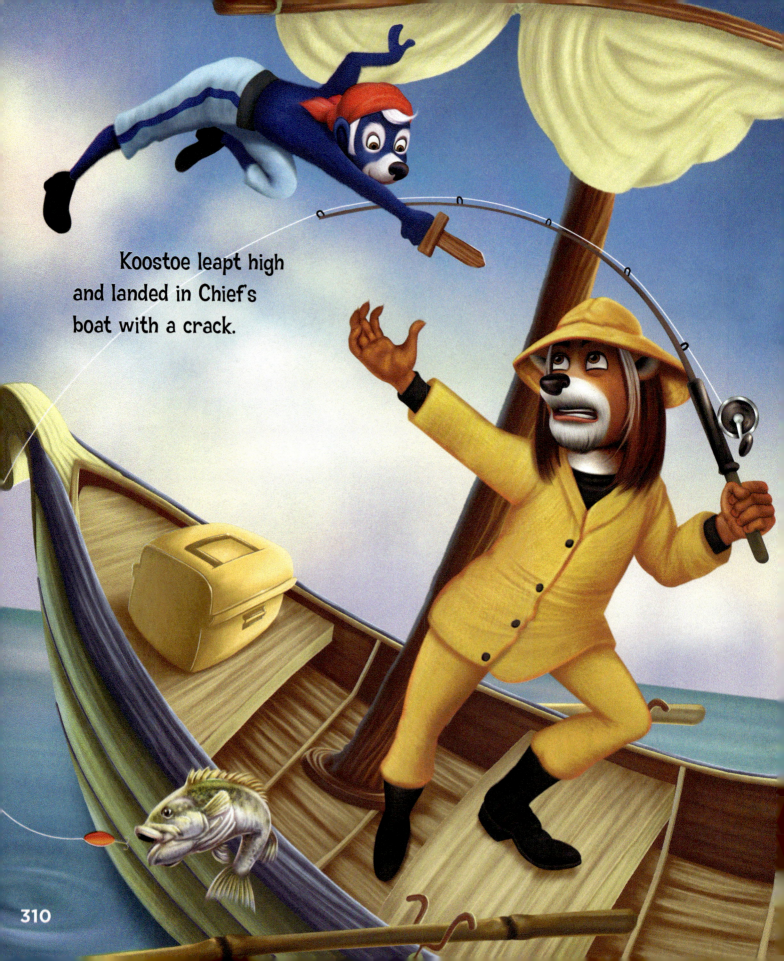

Koostoe leapt high and landed in Chief's boat with a crack.

"Oh, dear," said Chief. Koostoe's sword had poked a hole in the boat!

Koostoe helped drag Chief's boat ashore. "I don't think I should be a pirate anymore." Koostoe said. "They're fun to read about, but I don't like stealing or trying to be mean."

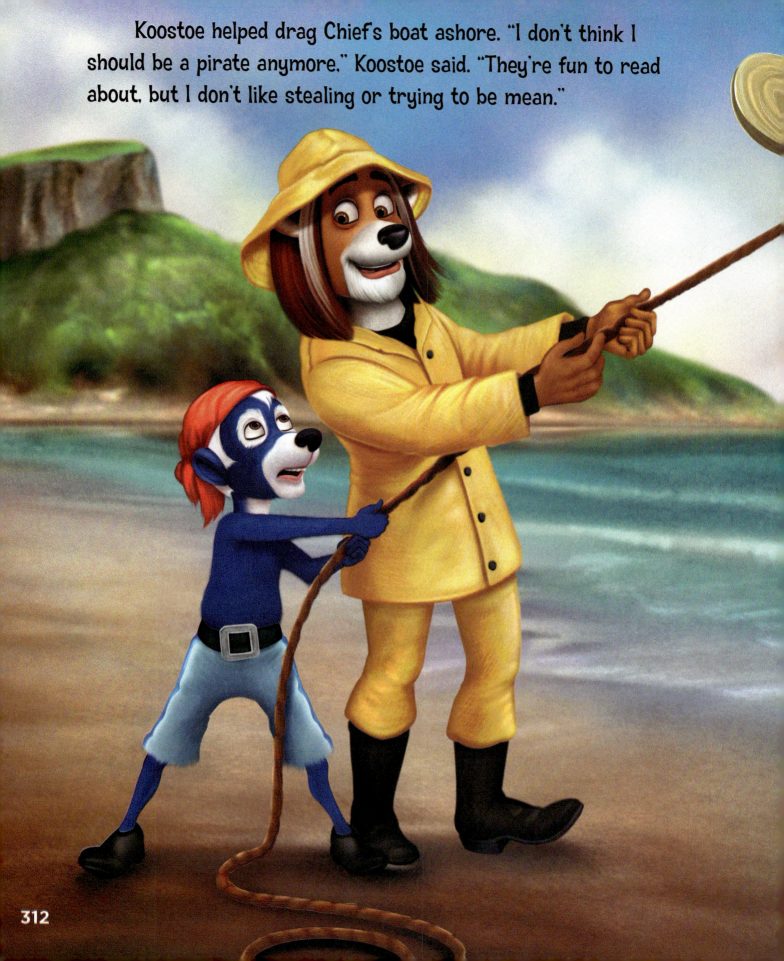

"I am glad to hear that," said Chief. "What made you want to be a pirate in the first place?"

"I like looking for treasure," explained Koostoe. "Plus, I really like sailing. That's another big part of being a pirate."

"There are other jobs where you get to sail," remarked Chief. "Perhaps you should focus on one of those."

"But if I don't become a pirate," replied Koostoe, "how will I find any treasure?"

Chief simply replied, **"Treasure comes in many forms."**

Koostoe did not understand what Chief meant, but he decided to take his advice. Koostoe studied hard and worked at the docks. In time, he saved enough money to build a small ship of his own.

Koostoe was quite proud of his ship, and he liked being its captain. *But I never found any treasure,* he often thought.

One day, an old friend came to visit.
It was Dewey!

"Ever since I became the town librarian," Dewey said, "I've been reading about the sea around Midlandia. I've learned a lot about it, but I've never had a chance to really be on the sea. Could you take me out on your ship?"

"Of course," replied Koostoe.

Koostoe sailed with Dewey all day. They saw little islands nearby, schools of swimming fish, and even a pod of dolphins. Koostoe enjoyed the trip....
But it's no treasure hunt, he thought.

When they returned to the docks, Dewey shook Koostoe's hand. "Thank you!" said Dewey. "I will always treasure the memories from today."

Koostoe's ears perked up. "Treasure? Where?"

Dewey pointed to his heart. "The treasure is right in here," he said. "Today was one of the best days of my life. A day like this is more precious than gold or jewels."

Koostoe finally understood what Chief had meant. Treasure did not have to be buried in the sand. It could be anything that someone values, such as a happy memory, the great feeling Koostoe got from helping his friend, or even....

"A starfish!" cried Wilda. "This will be perfect for my saltwater aquarium."

"I just knew that you would like it," said Koostoe.
"Thank you so much, Koostoe!" said Wilda. "You are a real treasure."
To which Koostoe simply replied, "Treasure comes in many forms."

Discussion Questions

What sorts of hobbies or interests do you have?
Can you think of any jobs that involve your interests?

Name a person you admire. What does he or she do for a job?
What would you like to do for a job when you grow up?

THE PIRATE KOOSTOE

Revised edition. First printing, January 2012.
Copyright 2020 © Lincoln Learning Solutions. All rights reserved.
294 Massachusetts Avenue
Rochester, PA 15074
Visit us on the web at http://www.lincolnlearningsolutions.org.
Midlandia® is a registered trademark of Lincoln Learning Solutions.

Edited by Ashley Mortimer
Midlandian Map by Danielle Caruso

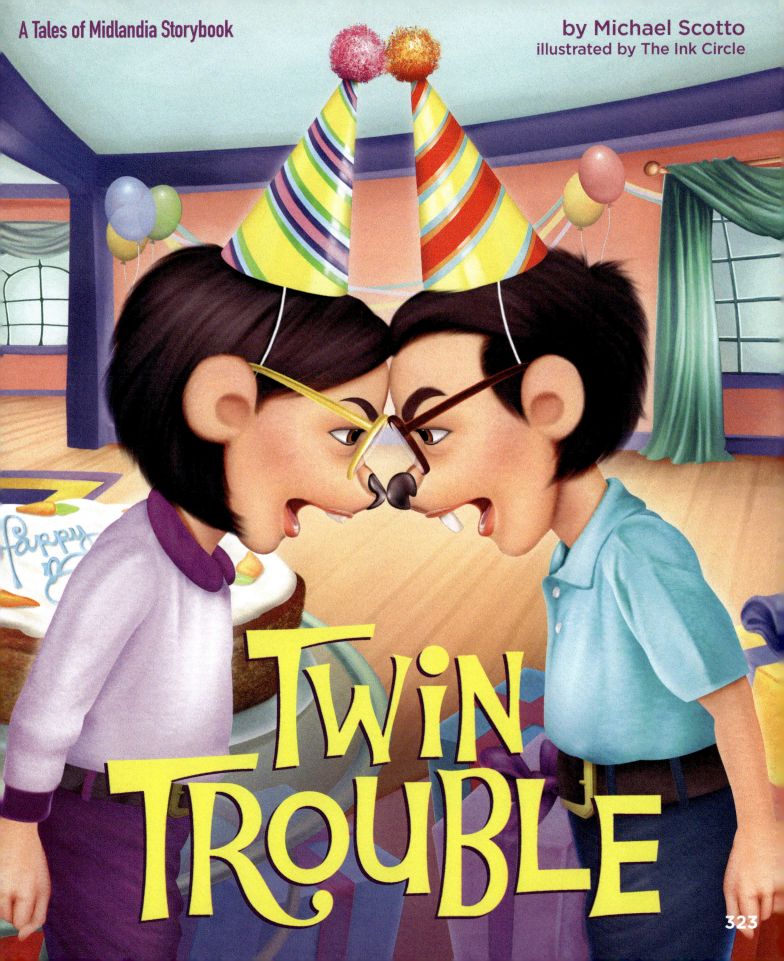

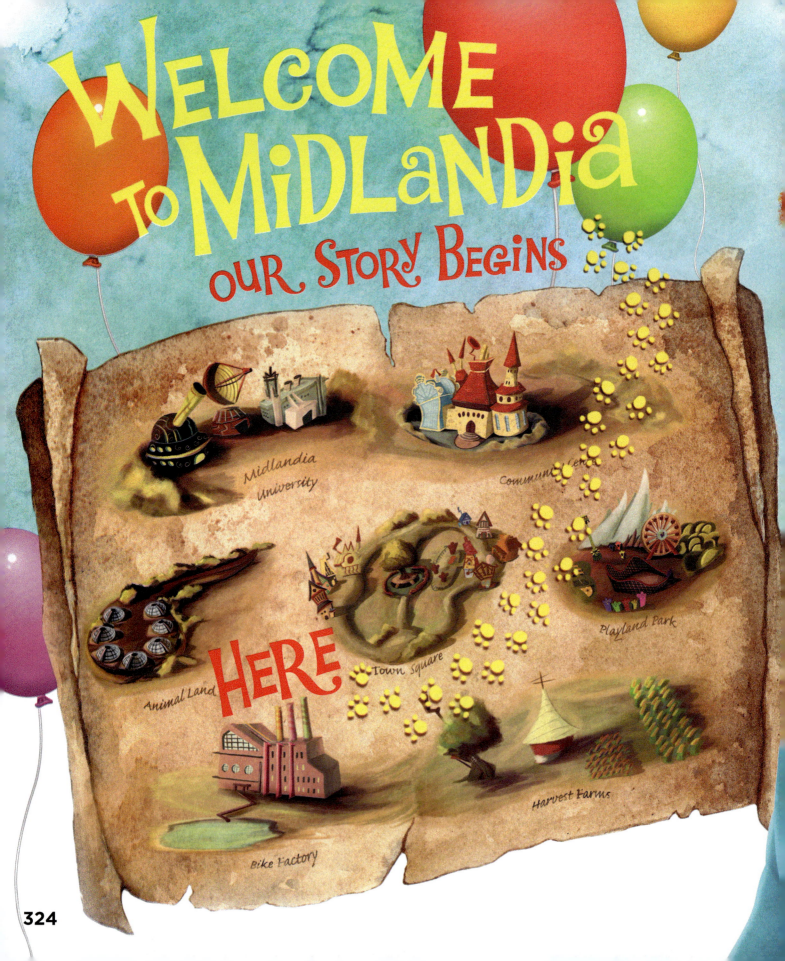

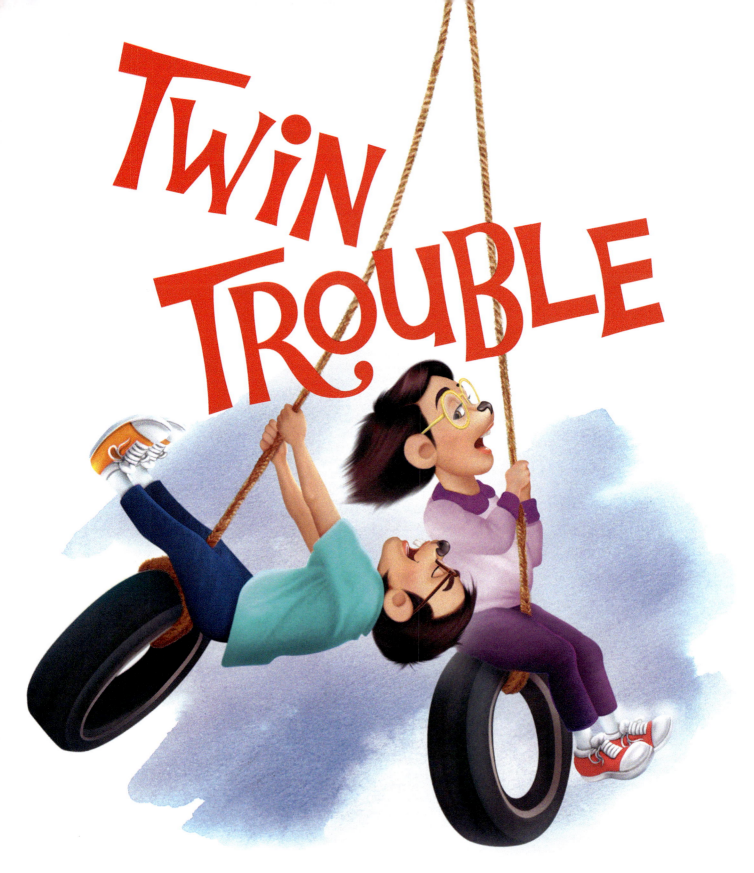

Brushy and Fixit were brother and sister. But they were a unique kind of brother and sister: **They were twins!**

These siblings were alike in many ways.

"We have the exact same smile, sis!" Brushy said.

"We are both the same height," Fixit noted. **"Isn't that cool?"**

But like many brothers and sisters, Brushy and Fixit argued a lot. When they were younger, it seemed like they did nothing but fight.

At home: "Your hair can wait," Brushy said. "I still need to floss!" "It'll be next week before you're done!" Fixit complained.

At the playground: "Watch it!" Fixit cried. "You almost broke my glasses!"

"Then you should keep your glasses out of my way," Brushy replied.

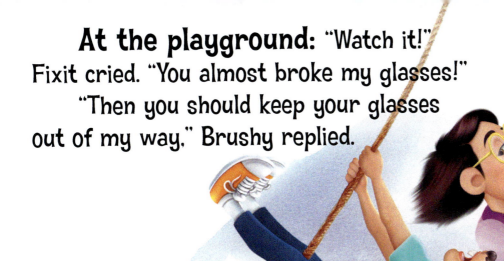

Even at the theater: "Oww, stop poking my ribs!" Brushy hissed.

"I'm not poking your ribs, silly," Fixit whispered. "I'm poking your sternum!"

Just like every brother and sister, Brushy and Fixit had their ups and their downs. But no one in Midlandia had been prepared for their biggest fight.

It had happened at the twins' birthday party. They had just reached the age where Midlandians began to decide what to do as grown-ups.

As Chief Tatupu served the carrot cake, Brushy took Fixit aside. "I have exciting news!" Brushy told her. "I have decided what I want to do for a job."

Ding-ding-ding! Fixit clinked a fork against her glass of birthday punch. "When Midlandians grow up, we each get to choose what job we want," she said. "I've made my choice. **I want to be a doctor!**"

Everyone in the crowd clapped...but Brushy only scowled.

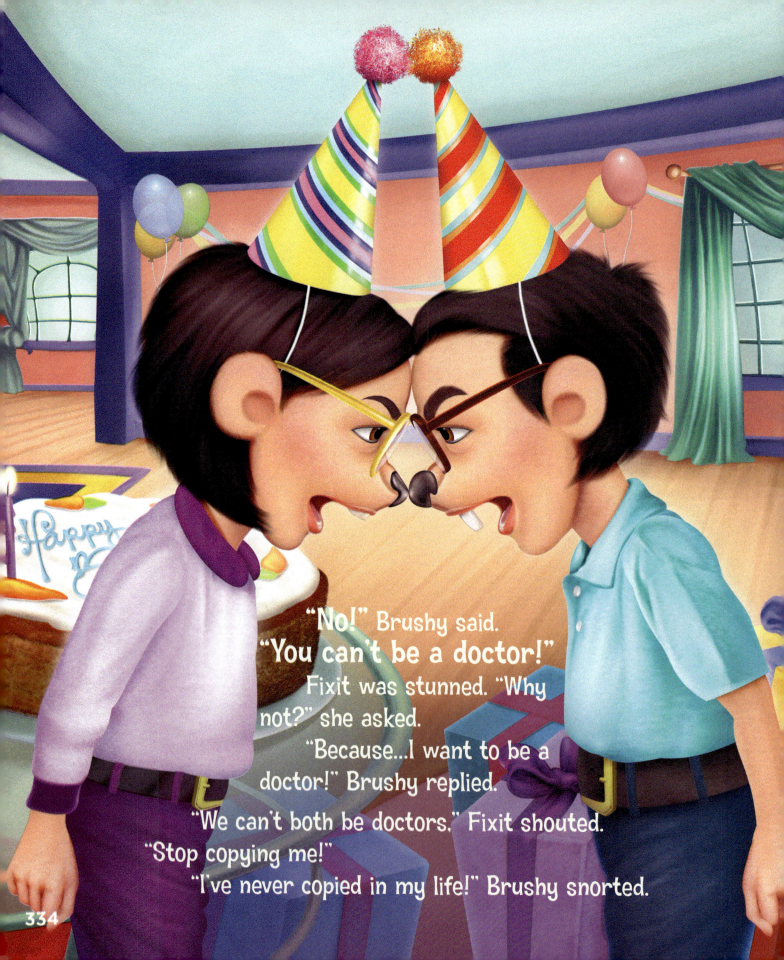

"No!" Brushy said. "You can't be a doctor!"

Fixit was stunned. "Why not?" she asked.

"Because...I want to be a doctor!" Brushy replied.

"We can't both be doctors," Fixit shouted. "Stop copying me!"

"I've never copied in my life!" Brushy snorted.

The twins paid Chief no mind.
"I said I wanted to be a doctor first," Fixit argued.
"Only because I let you speak first!" Brushy cried. "You've made a real mess of things now."
"**You want a mess?**" Fixit asked. She dug her hand into their birthday cake and rubbed a piece right in Brushy's face! "**That's a mess.**"

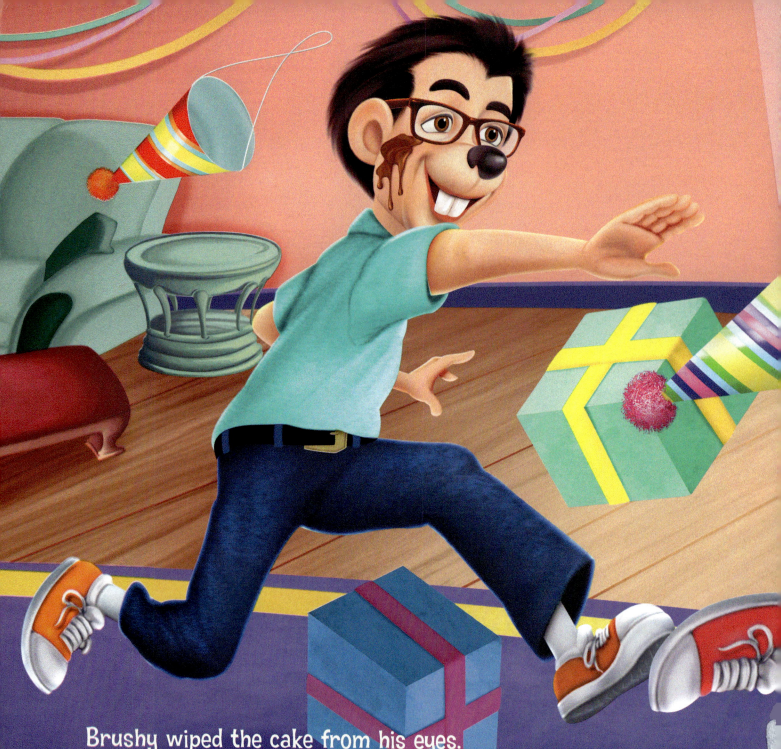

Brushy wiped the cake from his eyes.
"**Two can play at this game**," he declared.
The twins chased each other around the room, throwing cake and anything else they could get their hands on.
"Oh!" Fixit screamed. "**You're the worst brother ever!**"

I have to stop this before someone gets hurt! Chief thought. As Chief ran toward the fighting twins, Brushy lifted the punch bowl over his head.

"**How about a bath?**" Brushy said, and he dumped the whole bowl onto Fixit.

"**Ack, you punched me!**" Fixit cried.

Brushy tossed the empty bowl behind him...and it bonked Chief right on the head!

"**Ouch!**" he yelped. "**My noggin!**"

"Look what you did now, you big meanie!" Fixit yelled at her brother.

"That is enough!" Chief said, and he grabbed each twin by the collar to hold them apart. "**This party is over, everyone.**"

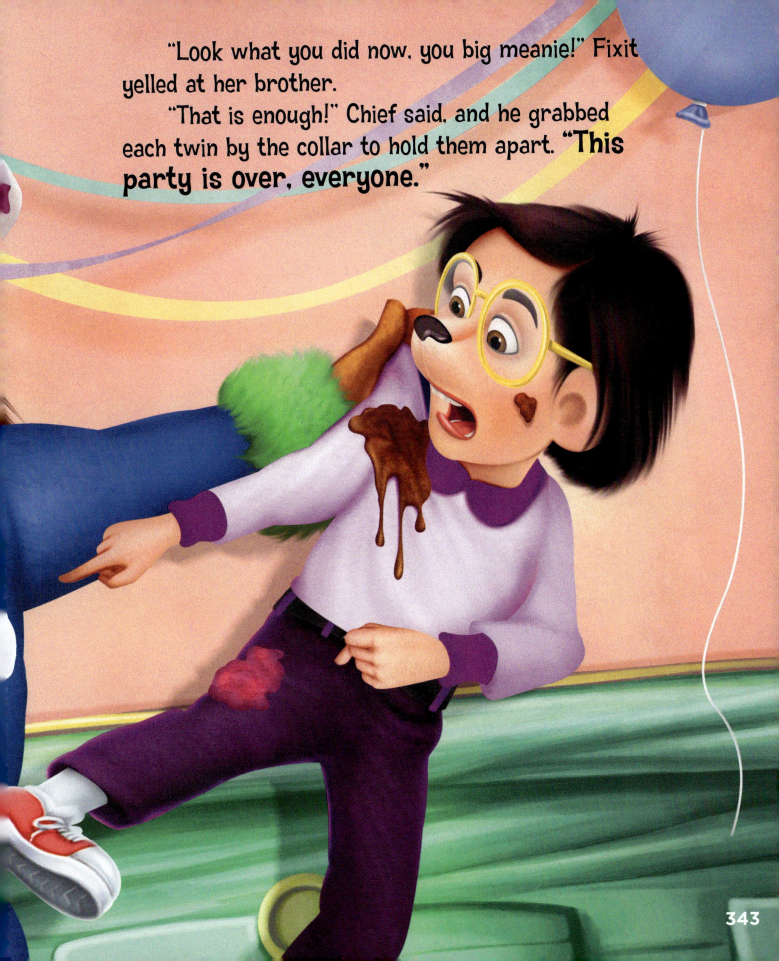

While Brushy mopped up the food fight, Fixit got Chief some ice and a bandage for the bump on his head.

"You need to stop this fighting," Chief told the twins.

"I try to get along with Fixit," Brushy huffed, "but sometimes, I get so mad at her!"

"I get mad at Brushy, too," Fixit said.

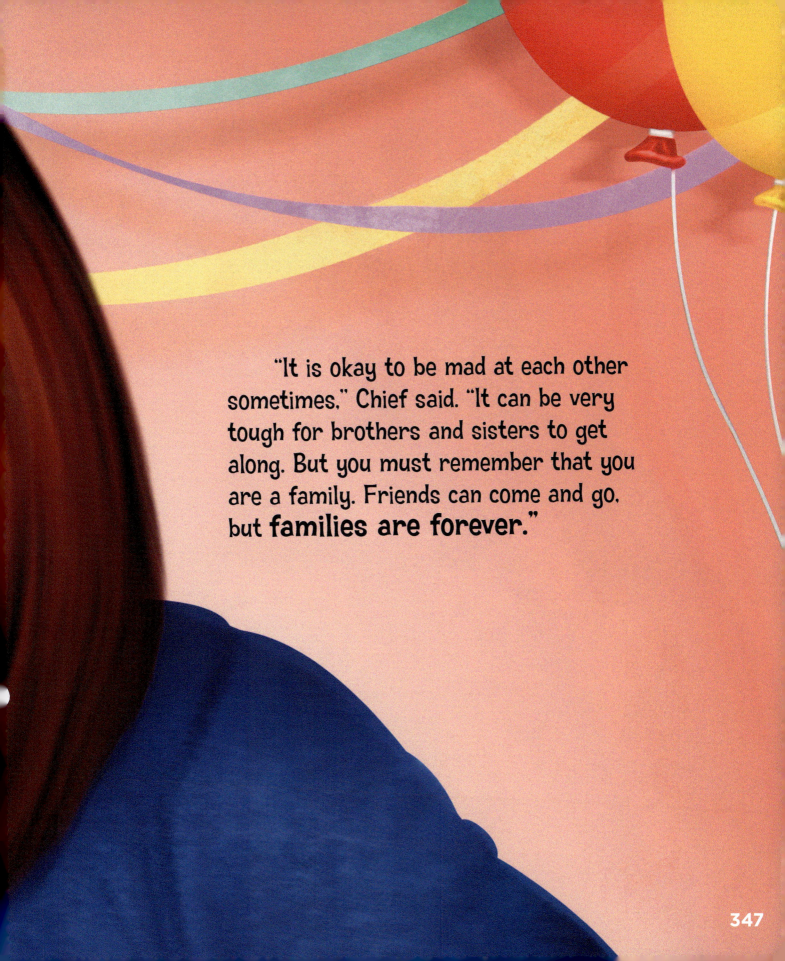

"It is okay to be mad at each other sometimes," Chief said. "It can be very tough for brothers and sisters to get along. But you must remember that you are a family. Friends can come and go, but **families are forever.**"

"I'm sorry for starting a fight with you," Brushy told Fixit.

"I'm sorry for saying you were a bad brother," Fixit told Brushy.

"This is more like it," Chief said. "It is always better to calmly share your feelings rather than yell or fight. Now, let us try to solve this doctor problem."

After a long talk, the twins found an answer. Perhaps they could both become doctors after all! At the University of Midlandia, Fixit and Brushy studied what interested each of them most. Fixit learned about bones, bumps, and bruises, while Brushy focused on teeth and tartar.

Once the twins finished school, Fixit became known as Doc Fixit. She used her skills to bandage, treat, and cure any Midlandian who needed her. **As for Brushy...**

...Brushy became a unique kind of doctor.
"**I'm a dentist!**" he exclaimed.
As a dentist, Brushy made sure that every smile in Midlandia stayed clean and sparkly.

From then on, the twins worked side by side. Fixit kept bodies healthy, and Brushy kept teeth healthy.

"May I borrow a tongue depressor, sis?" Brushy asked.

"Of course," Fixit replied. "We're a team."

"We're more than just a team," Brushy said. "We're a family!"

Discussion Questions

Do you have any brothers or sisters?
How are you similar to your other family members?
How are you different?

Have you ever had trouble getting along with someone?
How did you try to solve your problems?

TWIN TROUBLE

Revised edition. First printing, January 2008.
Copyright 2020 © Lincoln Learning Solutions. All rights reserved.
294 Massachusetts Avenue
Rochester, PA 15074
Visit us on the web at http://www.lincolnlearningsolutions.org.
Midlandia® is a registered trademark of Lincoln Learning Solutions.

Edited by Ashley Mortimer
Character design by Evette Gabriel
Environmental design by Joshua Perry